SUNSHINE
for the
HUMOROUS
LATTER-DAY
SAINT
SOUL

Parley —
Enjoy & keep Smiling!
Love
Sis Zowan
11-04

SUNSHINE

for the

HUMOROUS
LATTER-DAY
SAINT
SOUL

EAGLE GATE

SALT LAKE CITY, UTAH

We acknowledge copyright holders whose stories or poems we may have included but with whom we were unable to make personal contact. Other works are in public domain. If any acknowledgments have been overlooked, please notify the publisher and omissions will be rectified in future editions.

Library of Congress Cataloging-in-Publication Data

Sunshine for the humorous Latter-day Saint soul.
    p.   cm.
Includes bibliographical references.
    ISBN 1-57008-799-7 (pbk.)
    1. Church of Jesus Christ of Latter-day Saints—Humor.   2. Church of Jesus Christ of Latter-day Saints—Anecdotes.   I. Eagle Gate.

BX8638 .S89 2002
289.3'32'0207—dc21   2002002443

Printed in the United States of America   18961
R. R. Donnelley and Sons, Harrisonburg, VA

10   9   8   7   6

Contents

Love and Laughter

We're All in This Together

Families Are Forever . . . Is That Some Kind of Threat?

Out of the Mouths of Babes

Misunderstandings, Mistakes, and Merriment

Oh, Sure, It's Funny Now . . .

Preface

*W*hat makes something humorous is not always easy to explain. Sometimes it is the unexpected. We assume a story or a joke is leading to a certain place, and when it suddenly ends up somewhere else, the little jolt makes us smile or chuckle. Sometimes outlandish exaggerations make us laugh, a comedic device used so well by Mark Twain. We are also amused when someone we think of as sophisticated makes a blunder, which is the technique Victor Borge used so skillfully. When children make innocent statements that reflect an understanding they couldn't possibly possess, we smile behind our hands. "Kids say the darndest things."

So long as they don't cause permanent damage or irreparable harm, we find humor in the bizarre predicaments of other people and even ourselves. We smile or laugh at situations that are universally embarrassing or that reveal our vulnerabilities.

One theory has it that when a General Authority of the Church tells a story that is even only mildly funny, we laugh inordinately because it seems slightly out of character. We experience a release of tension as we discover our leaders are also human and not so inaccessible as we might have thought.

Though the Lord has warned against loud laughter, it is to remind us that we are to take seriously the doctrine of the kingdom and to not take lightly sacred things (see D&C 88:117–21). In fact, the Bible tells us there is "a time to laugh" (Ecclesiastes 3:4). Joseph Smith described himself as having a "native cheery temperament" (Joseph Smith—History 1:28) and reportedly enjoyed a humorous story. As you will be reminded in this volume, latter-day prophets have endeared themselves to us through the use of appropriate humor.

Our ability to laugh is a great gift. It is one of the things that "enliven[s] the soul" (D&C 59:19), and it refreshes us, relieves tension, and helps us better cope with our challenges.

We hope you will find in this collection of 101 short pieces much that will lighten your mood, brighten your day, and bring a smile to your face.

A Time to
Laugh

When Zucchini Happens . . .

JOSEPH WALKER

$\mathcal{S}$o I'm walking into the office one fall morning, minding my own business, when all of a sudden I turn the corner and there it is, sitting on my chair. Waiting. Lingering. Lurking.

"Oh, goody," I say, facetiously. "Zucchini."

"Isn't that nice?" says Marie, the irrepressibly upbeat person in the next office. "Somebody left zucchini for everyone!"

Ever notice how nobody actually *gives* you zucchini? At least, not in the same way they give you corn or apples or tomatoes. I mean, if someone wants to give you a few fresh, juicy peaches off their tree, they walk right up and hand them to you. You know—as though they're proud. As though they think you'll be pleased. They have confidence you're not going to run screaming into the night at the sight of their gift.

But with zucchini, they leave it and skulk away in a cowardly fashion. No note. No calling card. And no fingerprints. Zucchini is the abandoned orphan of the vegetable kingdom.

3

"Yeah—nice," I say. "Who should we . . . *thank* for this . . . *gift?*"

"Oh, I don't know," Marie says. "You know how it is with zucchini."

Of course I do. Zucchini is the perfect crime. It's quiet. It's lethal. And it's absolutely untraceable. That's because nobody actually grows it. At least, not on purpose. It just . . . happens. Like weeds. Or Chernobyl.

"So . . . what are you going to do with yours?" I ask.

"I'll just do what I always do with zucchini," she says.

"Yeah," I say, knowingly. "Me, too." By nightfall my zucchini is sleeping with the fishes.

Next morning I step into the office gingerly, afraid of what might be there waiting for me. I peek around the corner. No zucchini. But there is a slice of brown bread on a white napkin sitting on my desk. I eye it suspiciously. I pick it up. I smell it. It smells wonderful. I take a bite. It *is* wonderful!

"Who made the banana nut bread?" I ask, sinking my teeth into another mouthful.

Marie confesses. "Only it isn't banana nut bread," she says. "It's zucchini bread."

I stop chewing. "No way! This couldn't be zucchini. It's so . . . so . . . ."

"Good?" she offers.

"Yeah—good!" I exclaim. "But I hate zucchini!"

"So do I," Marie admits. "And I used to hate it when people gave me zucchini."

"*Abandon,*" I correct her. "People don't *give* zucchini; they *abandon* it. And zucchini isn't something you *receive;* it's something that *happens* to you."

4

"Whatever. One day I decided that there wasn't anything I could do to keep . . . well, to keep zucchini from happening to me. So I found this great recipe for zucchini bread, and now I actually look forward to zucchini season."

I take another bite of bread. Still wonderful. But I can't help wondering: "How could anything so tasty come from something so distasteful?"

"It's a fact of life," she says, philosophically. "You mix effort with creativity, and you can turn almost anything around."

"Even zucchini?"

"Hey, zucchini happens," she says, handing me another slice of bread. "But the way I see it, when life hands you a zucchini, make zucchini bread!"

Or in other words, never look an abandoned zucchini in the mouth.

When Several Days Attack You at Once

JANENE BAADSGAARD

I should have had the good sense to go back to bed when I woke up and remembered I had a dentist appointment later that morning. But naïve optimist that I am, I crawled out of bed anyway, tripped over my husband's shoes, and hit my head on the closet door.

I should have realized what kind of day I was in for when icicles formed on my teeth during a frigid shower because my teenagers had used all the hot water.

I should have seen it coming when my baby screamed all morning while I was hurrying to get ready, except when I held her and lovingly sang, "Booga-booga Baadsgaard baby . . . Booga-booga bye. If you don't stop screaming now . . . your mommy thinks she'll die."

I should have seen it coming when I hopped into the white station wagon and discovered that the battery was dead because Joseph and Jacob had been playing monsters-in-the-dark on the backseat the night before and left the dome light on.

I should have understood what lay ahead when I was forced to drive the green Baadsgaard Bomber. This is the family car without a reliable heat source. If you don't want to turn into a polar bear while driving somewhere, you have to plug in the cigarette lighter, take it out when it's hot, then wave it frantically around in the air.

I should have conceded defeat when I arrived at the dentist's office and they regretfully told me that the heating system had broken down, so would I please leave my coat on.

"Now this might pinch a little bit," my dentist said later as he plunged a six-foot needle into my jawbone. "That should make you feel better. We'll let that get good and numb, and I'll be back in a jiffy."

But when the man in white came back about two hours later and my cheek wasn't even tingly, I got the needle again. My jaw never did go numb, but my nose went completely dead, proving once and for all my husband's claim that my brain's not wired correctly.

As I sat in the dentist chair with a frozen nose, jackhammer hammering away on an unfrozen tooth, spit drooling down my chin, a chunk of old filling stuck in the back of my throat, and an air vacuum sucking out my tongue, I remembered that I'd forgotten to turn off the stove.

The car started making a funny knocking noise during the drive home just before a rock flipped up and cracked the windshield we had replaced only three weeks earlier. The only bumper sticker I saw read, "Life is hard, then you die."

7

All I can say, Mom, . . . is that living one day at a time is good advice, unless the day you happen to be living feels like a whole week.

OD'd on Shrimp

TOM PLUMMER

*O*ne night after a shrimp dinner at the Ling Ling Panda, Louise broke into hives. We were at a university gala dance when, in the middle of a slow number, I noticed she was scratching her wrist. We would dance a few steps, then she'd free her right hand and scratch her left wrist behind my head. Then she would take her left hand from my neck and scratch her right wrist.

"I've got hives," she said. "They're breaking out on my hands and arms. Look." Sure enough, large red welts were forming.

"Do you want to leave?" I asked.

"No, let's dance a few more and see how it goes," she said.

I didn't argue. We put cheeks together and danced on. After two or three numbers she said, "We'd better go. I have a serious problem."

By the time we reached home, large welts had formed all over her body. It was nearly 11:00 P.M., and the pharmacies were closed. I called the doctor's emergency number. "This isn't a big problem," he assured me. "Go down to Smith's (the twenty-four-hour grocery store) and get a bottle of Benadryl. Have her drink a quarter cup. It'll stop the hives and she'll sleep like a baby." Both were true. The hives subsided, and she slept until noon.

We were not sure what had caused the hives. We suspected the shrimp, possibly the MSG in the shrimp, but quite possibly something unrelated. After that, Louise ate shrimp periodically—especially at Chinese restaurants. For a long time there were no more allergic reactions. Then, maybe one time in five, she would break out. We kept Benadryl around, and when a hive or two emerged, she'd take the usual quarter cup and pass out for the night. "I like my shrimp with a Benadryl chaser," she would say to friends.

One night we went to China Lily's with our good friends Al and Ginny Wirthlin. They like to order a lot of different foods and share dishes. I enjoy that, too, but Louise is very clear about what she wants. She wants what she orders, and she doesn't want to share. "If I had wanted your Szechuan beef, I'd have ordered it for myself," she told Al. "I just want shrimp, and I want all of it." So Al, Ginny, and I ordered food to share, and Louise ordered shrimp for herself.

Maybe the cook was drunk that night. Her plate was piled high—at least two dozen shrimp. Louise squealed and clasped her hands. "Oh, goody. I'm going to eat every last one." While the rest of us ate communally, Louise gorged on the shrimp. "Boy, was that good," she said as she finished the last piece. "I'm glad I didn't have to share."

For a short while there were no aftereffects. We sat in the restaurant and talked; then the Wirthlins took us home. As their car pulled away, Louise grabbed my arm and said, "My tongue is swelling up." She guzzled Benadryl from the bottle, which didn't improve the condition. Her breathing was becoming labored.

"Come on," I said, "let's get you to the emergency room. Tell the doctor you OD'd on shrimp."

When we arrived at the hospital, her breathing was a bit better. "Let's just sit here in the parking lot for a few minutes," she said. "I think it's going away." After a half hour she said, "I think we can go now."

As we lay snuggling in bed that night, she said, "You think I'm stupid, don't you?"

"No," I said. "You just OD'd." Then I laughed.

The next day she called the Wirthlins to tell them what had happened. "It's God's punishment," Al said. "You wouldn't share."

Self-esteem

MARILYNNE LINFORD

A few years ago I wrote a book on self-esteem.
I felt insecure in my new role as author. I gave one of the
first copies to a friend whose approval I needed. When
I hadn't heard from her in more than a week, I called to
see if she had read it yet. She said she had finished the
book and thought it contained some helpful things.
"But," she said, "I think there is a problem."

"What's that?" I worried.

"Well," she said, "I think you may become conceited.
I've put myself in charge of keeping you humble." I had
hoped for a battery charge, but I got drained instead.

A week later another friend called. "I just finished
reading your book," she said enthusiastically, "and I just
had to call to tell you it has changed my life."

"That's wonderful," I said. "What in the book was so
significant?"

"Well . . ." She thought. "It wasn't anything specific. It's
just, well, it's, well . . . Now you don't intimidate me anymore." Some more of the charge on my battery was gone.

A few weeks after that, the company that published

the book had their advertising agent call me. She said it was possible that someone, sometime, might interview me on radio or television. Since I had no experience with such matters, they wanted me to have a practice videotaping session. They had arranged for an anchorwoman to interview me and give me pointers, and they were mailing me a book that would help me prepare.

When the book came, I studied it carefully. I did exactly as it said. I chose my clothes according to the instructions about what to wear on TV. I studied the makeup and hairdo sections. I had my hair cut and wore extra makeup. I had my husband give me practice questions until I felt I could at least make a decent response. At the appointed time I arrived at the advertising agent's office. I was introduced to the anchorwoman, two agents, and a cameraman. The anchorwoman immediately began the interview. After about twenty minutes of questions and answers, she said she'd seen enough.

"Well," she began, "I have to admit that you surprised me. You look so plain, kind of mousy; you answered better than I would have expected by just looking at you. But don't worry. I think we can fix you up. Do you have any classy clothes? Any of us here would be glad to go shopping with you to find one outfit that would be suitable. Also, is this the only way you do your hair? My hairdresser, Valentino, would be glad to show you some flattering styles. And Maria, my makeup artist, could help you a lot. Actually," she concluded optimistically, "I think you could be rather pretty." After more of the same, I thanked them and said I was going home to read a good book on self-esteem.

The Geezer in the Glass

JOSEPH WALKER

$\mathcal{S}$o I'm walking across the college campus, and I'm feeling very . . . how shall I say . . . collegiate.

I'm wearing jeans, a sweatshirt, and tennis shoes, so I'm certainly dressed for the part. My bookbag is slung over my shoulder, and my hair is badly in need of a trim. Strolling among the students it all begins to feel familiar, as though I've been there before—which, of course, I have. Sixteen years ago, to be precise. Only from this side of my eyeglasses it doesn't feel like it's been that long. Everything looks the same. I'm home again. I'm Joe College. I *belong.*

Except for one thing. I can't remember if the library is on this side of the bookstore, or if it's over there. I stop at a campus map to refresh my memory. Suddenly I notice this cute girl giving me . . . you know . . . The Look. At first I think maybe I'm mistaken, so I look away. Maybe we had a class together. After all, it was only a few years ago . . .

I glance back. *Definitely* The Look. She begins to cross toward me. Poor thing. How can I let her down easily?

"Excuse me, sir," she says.

Sir???

She continues: "I couldn't help noticing—"

"Yes?" I interrupt anxiously.

"You look a little lost. May I help you?"

I recognize her tone of voice, and I'm relieved and devastated all at once. It's that same condescending tone we all use when communicating with the very young.

And the very old.

"I think I've figured it out—thanks anyway," I say, fighting off an overwhelming urge to call her "dearie." She turns to leave, but I stop her. "You know, you look awfully familiar to me," I say. "Didn't we have a class together a few years ago?"

She eyes me warily. "I don't know. When were you here?"

"My last year was 1978."

She smiles at me kindly. "I don't think so," she says, turning to leave. "In 1978, I was in the first grade."

For some reason, there's a little less bounce in my step as I trudge wearily to the library. Walking past the bookstore, I notice in the glass window a reflection of this old guy wearing jeans, a sweatshirt, and tennis shoes. *What is it,* I wonder, *Geezer Day or something?*

Then I study the reflection more carefully. The geezer in the glass is me. I keep forgetting what the years have done to me. In my mind I'm still the svelte sophomore who prowled the campus sixteen years before. In fact, I don't feel any differently today than I did in high school. But then I step on the basketball court and try to keep up with the 8th graders I'm coaching, or I try to follow

15

my fifteen-year-old daughter's peculiar brand of logic ("It's okay to wear shorts in the middle of winter because everyone does it, so nobody is any colder than anyone else"), and I realize that I *am* different. My body is different, my mind works through problems differently, and many of my values and perspectives are vastly changed from what they used to be.

And that isn't such a bad thing, is it? Life is seasonal, and the ebb and flow of the seasons of our lives brings about change—physically, spiritually, mentally, emotionally, and socially. Not only would life be boring if everything always stayed the same, but there would also be precious little progress. And so we age. And we change. And, hopefully, we grow.

Which may be a long-winded way of justifying the physical deterioration I have allowed to happen to me through the years. But it is also a way of looking at life, accepting its seasonal variances, and embracing the wondrous opportunity of change.

And while you're at it, learning to recognize and appreciate the geezer in the glass.

Meeting Miss America

JOANN PETERSON

While working as an editor, my husband received an unexpected assignment to work with Sharlene Wells (Hawkes) on a book she was writing. Sharlene had been named Miss America in 1985, and she wanted to describe that experience and some of the opportunities that followed. She told Richard that in her travels as Miss America and later as a sports analyst and color commentator for ESPN, she had frequent opportunities to meet prominent people who often asked her about her religious beliefs. Her book would show how Latter-day Saints can live in the world without becoming part of the world.

After meeting Sharlene for the first time and spending a couple of hours with her, Richard came home from work, anxious to talk about the thrill it had been to meet a former Miss America. He admitted that he was initially intimidated by her but had quickly found her to be as gracious and friendly as she is beautiful.

He told me she had been born in Paraguay and because of her father's career had spent most of her childhood in Mexico and South America. She had described how as a lone Latter-day Saint, she had often had to defend her beliefs when they were challenged by schoolmates and others. She had also become fluent in Spanish and learned to play the Paraguayan harp.

I remembered her playing the harp in the Miss America Pageant and was intrigued. "What else did you learn?" I asked.

"Well," he said, "the biggest thing I learned is that it's impossible for me to hold my stomach in for two straight hours."

Who's Next?

SHAUNA GIBBY

We have a condominium development in our ward. Most of the residents in these condos are retired couples. They add a lot of depth and experience to our ward but also give us more elderly members than in most wards. We had had two or three weeks in a row in which we had a funeral. During Relief Society, one of the counselors (who happened to be one of the condo residents) was conducting. She explained that a sign-up sheet was going around for food assignments for the funeral that week. She then said, "If it is full by the time it gets to you, just sign the bottom and we'll use you next week."

The Optimist

UNKNOWN

The optimist fell ten stories.
At each window bar
He shouted to his friends:
"All right so far."

Home Improvement

TOM PLUMMER

$\mathscr{I}$ had never associated home improvement with venereal disease until we bought our first house. It was a narrow, tall structure with white siding, black shutters, and a black roof that rose steeply from the first to the third story. We found it by driving through neighborhoods we liked. It seemed to call to us.

"It looks like a crooked little Dutch house," Louise said. "It's darling." Its slight lean to the south made me nervous, but her clasped hands told me she was charmed. "But what about the paint on the roof around the dormer?" she asked. "I hate that."

"I can fix that in a jiffy," I said.

"The outside needs paint," she said. The paint on the siding was peeling away in large strips. "Can we paint it?"

"No problem," I said. "I know how to paint a house. I'll just scrape it down, prime it, and put on a new coat."

I went to the door and asked the owner the price.

"Twenty-three thousand, five hundred dollars," she

21

said. That was exactly what we could afford. It was too good to be true.

"Can we just run through?" I asked.

The interior was more intimidating. A filthy, sculpted, yellow carpet from past generations covered the living- and dining-room floors. The walls were scratched and dirty; the kitchen countertop was a worn, dark red linoleum; the carpet was rubber-backed, dirty, mottled red and black. Most bizarre were the stalactites hanging everywhere from the ceilings—plaster spikes, like icicles, one to two inches long. Someone had tried to create a textured surface but had put the plaster on too wet and not wiped it down. The result was stalactites.

"I can knock those off in a couple of hours," I said to Louise, who was quite pale. "I just need a ladder and a scraper."

We made an offer on the spot.

"You have to take care of the ceilings first," Louise said. "I can't live with that for an hour."

I bought a ladder and a couple of scrapers. On the first swipe, the scraper bounced from tip to tip without knocking off a single one. They were hard as granite. I went back to the hardware store, bought heavy-duty scrapers with replacement blades, and swung again. I spent a full week, all day every day, scraping.

After six or seven days, my right elbow swelled to the size of a grapefruit. It was so sore I couldn't stand for even a bed sheet to touch it. My temperature rose to 103 degrees, and I ached all over. I lay in bed moaning. For two days, Louise kept ice packs on me to control the fever.

Finally I called our HMO program. "Dr. Muelleck has an opening tomorrow morning," the receptionist told me.

"Isn't someone available sooner?" I whined. "I want to die."

"Sorry," the voice on the other end said. "Tomorrow at 9:30 A.M. is the first available appointment. Everyone else is unavailable until next week."

Louise drove me to the clinic the next morning. I groaned all the way there—she has always accused me of having a low pain threshold—and eventually a nurse ushered me into an examination room.

Dr. Muelleck appeared. She was about six-foot-two, sinewy, with straight brown hair, maybe in her forties. With no greeting, she sat down on a stool opposite mine and said, "What's the trouble?" Her tone was cold and cranky. It told me she didn't want to be there.

I pointed to my enormous elbow. "My arm is killing me, and I've had a fever of 103 for three days. I can't eat or sleep."

Her severe expression turned savage. With no warning whatsoever, no hesitation, she took my ailing elbow in both hands and began to squeeze and twist it like she was wringing out a towel. "Does that hurt?" she asked.

I steeled my face to keep my mouth from twitching, although I wanted to writhe on the floor, and said in my coldest, deepest, calmest voice, "Lady, you're killing me."

"Then why aren't you screaming?" she asked.

I could feel sweat breaking out on my forehead. "Because I was taught never to scream in front of a woman," I said.

"Well," she said, recoiling for the next strike. "You've got gonorrhea."

I took a deep breath. "I don't have gonorrhea," I said.

"Yes, you do," she said. "You have gonorrhea."

"Can you get gonorrhea from a toilet seat?" I asked. That much I could remember from my high school health class.

"No, you can't," she said.

"Then I don't have gonorrhea," I said.

"Are you sure?"

"Yes, I'm sure."

"Then you have bursitis," she said.

"What's wrong?" Louise asked when I came out.

"I have gonorrhea," I said.

Once when I was telling this story to a group of friends in Minnesota, Grace Gregory, a woman in her late eighties, said, "I know that doctor. I know her. I took the bus to that very clinic for a physical examination. I was waiting in the little room for my doctor, and this Dr. Muelleck comes along. Do you know what she said to me? She is not my doctor, but she pokes her head in, sees me, and says, 'You have hardening of the arteries. You'll be dead in six months.' Then she walked off. She didn't even know me. Do you know what I did?"

"What?" I asked.

"Well, in six months, I got on the bus, went all the way across town to that clinic, walked right past the receptionist and down the hall to the examination rooms, and opened every door until I found Dr. Muelleck. She was with a patient. I said, 'You told me six months ago that I'd be dead now. Well, here I am, and I'm not dead.' Then I got on the bus and went home." Grace lived another fifteen years.

Just out of curiosity, I called my old HMO recently to see if Dr. Muelleck was still around. It's been more than twenty-five years since my encounter. "Do you have a Dr. Muelleck on the staff?" I asked.

"Yes, sir," the voice said. "Dr. Muelleck is now at our Fairview Clinic."

Over the years, my rancor toward Dr. Muelleck has receded, not because my heart has softened, but because I have become more grateful for what she did. A more competent doctor would not have given me the story that I so love to tell. Nor would Louise have her favorite opener—for times when social conversation lags: "Tom was diagnosed with gonorrhea."

God Save the King!

MARY ELLEN EDMUNDS

*W*hen Dad was a physician in Cedar City, in Southern Utah, he had a particular older woman as a patient who came frequently to his office with her adult son. Neither the mother nor the son seemed completely whole mentally. There were times when their behavior was unusual, as the time when the mother saw Dad on the street and slapped him on the back (with a "Hi, Doc!") so hard that she almost threw him into the ditch.

As I mentioned, this duo came to Dad's office frequently with various complaints, but perhaps mostly wanting someone to pay attention to them. One day when they arrived, Dad's nurse thought she'd be clever, and she sent a note in to Dad saying, "The Queen and the Prince are here." Dad peeked out to see that it was this particular mother and her son, and he wrote something on the note and passed it back to the nurse: "God save the King!"

A Moment of Fame

ROBERT FARRELL SMITH

A few years back, we were lucky enough to get Steve Young to make a pit stop in our city and say a few words to some gathered Saints. I owned the only LDS bookstore in the area, and I thought it would be great for the community and for business to help put the event together. Well, somehow, on the night of his appearance, I ended up with the honor of driving Steve around, and I even got to sit next to him on the stand.

The place was packed. People were crammed into every available inch of the chapel and overflow, and Steve of course did a fantastic job. When he sat down after his speech, the entire congregation just sat there, gaping at him in awe.

Well, I did what any insecure, spotlight-grabbing human being would do under the circumstances. I leaned over to Steve and quietly said, "If you put your arm around me and laugh like I just said something really funny, everyone here will think I'm cool."

Steve did his part and then some, adding a pat on the back for flair. Because of that small gesture, to this day people still bring me ideas and comments for me to pass along to my good friend, Steve Young.

Sometimes, I tell them how it really was.

Driving from a Wheelchair

ART E. BERG

*C*ritically injured in an automobile rollover, I was left a quadriplegic at age twenty-one. More than a year after leaving the hospital, I began to learn how to drive again.

I eventually purchased a minivan that had been equipped for my use. The van had a ramp to provide me access to the inside. Once inside, I simply rolled behind the steering wheel and locked my chair electronically into place.

I was out running some errands a few weeks later when some of my teenage impulses mysteriously returned. I was stopped at a traffic light when another minivan pulled up beside me. I eyed the van and driver. His van was the same make, model, and year as the one I was driving—with one major difference: I had the superior V6, fuel-injected model, and he didn't! I began to rev my engine just a little. He glanced over at me, noticed the smirk on my face, and revved his engine, too.

The light turned green, and we both accelerated. I slammed the accelerator from my hand controls to the floor, my tires chirped, and I sped through the inter-section. Suddenly, my wheelchair broke free from its electronic lock and immediately propelled itself straight to the back of my van. With the other driver pulling ahead and my vehicle without a driver, my van changed lanes. Pushing against the force of the moving van, I somehow made my way back to the steering wheel and slowly brought my vehicle to a stop. My racing days were over.

The van was convenient, but there was a measure of risk: my wheelchair was not nearly as prepared to absorb the impact of an accident as a permanent cap-tain's seat would be. My concern was what would hap-pen if I should one day be rear-ended. The force of the impact would throw my body backward, and the low back on my wheelchair would be inadequate to hold me in place.

One afternoon, while waiting at another traffic light, it happened. I heard a loud crash from behind as my body jerked backward. I had been rear-ended. My head was now resting on the floor behind where I had been seated. With my wheelchair still locked in place behind the steering wheel, my knees had caught under the dash, and so I was doing a perfect backbend that would make any gymnast envious.

About that time I noticed through the windows that the clouds were moving above me. Then I realized that it wasn't the clouds that were moving—it was me! With my hand off the hand-controlled brake, the van was rolling slowly through the heavily traveled intersection. Cars screeched to a halt to avoid hitting my vehicle. I could just imagine what the other drivers were thinking as they saw a driverless van going through a red light. Miraculously, again, I was able to pull myself back into an upright position. People were staring at me from all directions. I smiled and waved.

I come from a family of nine children, and I am the serious one! From the time I was a child, my family has used its sense of humor to handle any crisis. I am not sure I would have survived the emotional trauma of my injuries and the complications of my new life if it hadn't been for the wit, chuckles, laughs, and good-natured humor of my family.

"Welcome Back, Stupid!"

MARY ELLEN EDMUNDS

$\mathcal{I}$ remember a friend telling me about a journey he was making from Point A to Point B on a freeway one day, and he was in a great hurry. There was a section of the freeway that had not yet been completed. It seemed to him that they'd been working on it an awfully long time, and as he looked at it on his approach, it appeared that the only thing left to do was paint the lines. He reasoned that if he could get around the huge "Road Closed" signs and head on down the brand-new freeway, he wouldn't need lines—he'd be the only car on the road.

He managed that; he maneuvered his car around the signs and headed down the freeway, whipping along, feeling very clever.

But alas! As he got a couple of miles farther there was a section of overpass that had not yet been finished, and he had to make a U-turn and go all the way back.

Obviously he wasn't the only driver who had ever tried this very good idea. On the flip side of the huge "Road Closed" sign was this hand-lettered message: "Welcome back, stupid!"

Elevator Icebreaker

MARY ELLEN EDMUNDS

*O*ne place where I find it most challenging to speak up and reach out is on elevators. It seems like there's almost an unwritten law forbidding people to talk or laugh when they're on an elevator. Have you noticed that? Here is a group of friends, laughing and visiting, and then, almost as if they've been hit with an invisible wand as they step into the elevator, they hush. Everyone faces the closing doors and looks at whatever thing might be on the walls—like the last inspection Otis did, whoever he is. The "studied quietude" of the elevator is absolutely fascinating!

So I've tried for years to make myself interact with others on elevators. I'm sure my efforts aren't always appreciated, but often they result in fun and interesting encounters.

One day I got on an elevator and a man followed, and we were both using our good elevator manners, looking straight ahead and not speaking. He had some papers and was kind of shuffling them around a bit. My heart was pounding because I knew I wanted to break the silence in some way. I gathered courage and said, as pleasantly as I could, "Want to see my paper cut?"

It caught him *way* off guard, of course. I could see him fighting a smile, though, and I knew he was a goner. Once people begin to smile or laugh, the walls are gone, the pretense has fled, and wonderful things are about to happen. He responded, "Not really." "Good!" I almost shouted. "Because I don't really have one—I was just trying to make conversation."

Then he laughed out loud, and what a great time we had for the rest of our ride. He told me about a swell movie starring James Garner that all hinges on a paper cut! Apparently James Garner is captured by the enemy during the war, and they try to convince him that he's been in a deep coma for many years, and the war is over, and he's lost, so now he can reveal all that the Americans were *going* to do to try to win.

Just as he is about to spill it all, he feels his paper cut and realizes that it is the same day as when he got the cut, and he doesn't reveal anything.

What a difference as the man and I got off the elevator a few minutes later! We were chatting and laughing like old friends. I can't wait to see the movie.

Tent Failure

RANDAL WRIGHT

*W*hile serving as a member of a bishopric a few years ago, I was asked to accompany a group of Scouts on a river rafting trip in the Texas hill country. We were to camp on a Friday night and then spend all day Saturday on the river. Upon arriving at our campsite, the three other leaders and I started putting up a tent we had borrowed. No instructions were included, but since our group included two men holding master's degrees, one with a dental degree, and one a Ph.D., we weren't worried.

We soon discovered that the tent we had borrowed was defective. After all, if we couldn't figure out how to put it together, something must be wrong with the tent. We were somewhat puzzled, however, since all the pieces appeared to be included, and the tent looked almost new. For the next two hours we tried everything possible to get that tent up, without success. Finally, in total frustration, one of the leaders got out ropes and tied the tent off to several nearby trees, creating a makeshift shelter out of the canvas. When the Scouts came back from a short hike, they laughed and laughed at the mangled looking tent. It was very embarrassing for the leaders.

Most of the boys slept out under the stars that night, but wanting to be a united group of leaders, the four of us tried to sleep in our jerry-rigged shelter. In the middle of the night, one side of the tent collapsed on top of me. After finding my way out, I tried to sleep in my car the rest of the night. When morning dawned, we were all miserable because of lack of sleep.

As we were preparing to put the raft into the river, two college-aged young women drove up to a camping spot right beside ours and unloaded several items out of their car. I watched as they lifted a tent out of the trunk. What a coincidence! They had a tent exactly like ours. I couldn't help but laugh to myself, as we watched them prepare to assemble their tent. This was going to be good.

It was obvious that they had never put the tent up before because they constantly referred to the instructions. But working together, they had it completely up within ten minutes. It was then that I realized that there were no defective or missing parts in our borrowed tent.

I was hoping we could leave before the Scouts noticed the girls' tent, but it was too late. The boys gave it to us pretty good, and there was nothing we could do but take their taunts and teasing like men. Besides, those girls had essentially cheated as they put up their tent. They had followed the instructions. What's the challenge in that?

Alzheimer's Pop Quiz

TOM PLUMMER

A few years ago at Christmas we invented the Alzheimer's Pop Quiz, which has become our favorite game of attack. We wanted to buy some poinsettias from the local nursery, but neither of us could remember the word *poinsettia*. We kept saying things like "those Christmas plants with the red and green leaves," and "the plant that begins with a 'p' or 'r' or 'h.'"

Finally we decided to set out for the nursery hoping that we would remember the word before we got there. As we drove along, we tried various prompts and phonetic gimmicks, but to no avail. When we arrived, we still couldn't remember the name.

"I'm not going in until I can remember," Louise said. "You go ahead." But I was obsessed with the problem, too, so we drove around some more. Finally we came to a Sprouse-Reitz store that was going out of business. Only a teenage clerk was inside.

"Maybe we can find something in there with a picture and name on it," I said. I could see boxes decorated with flora that appeared to be poinsettias. Louise walked straight to the teenage clerk, grabbed him by the sleeve, and dragged him over to the boxes. The flora were indeed poinsettias. "What kind of plant is that?" she demanded.

He was as stupid as we were. "Duh, I don't know," he said. "A rose?"

"Dummy, that's not a rose," Louise said. She smacked him on the shoulder. "Give me a break." We roared out of the store, leaving the clerk baffled and confused.

Finally we gave up and went back to the nursery. Inside were long rows of green and red plants with the name "poinsettia" plastered all over the place. We could have spared ourselves the trouble.

The idea behind the Alzheimer's Pop Quiz as we now play it is to surprise the other person with a question that he or she could normally answer but can't answer on the spot, because he or she simply can't retrieve the information fast enough. The Alzheimer's Pop Quiz preys on the slower memory retrieval of middle-aged adults.

The quiz begins without warning. We're eating dinner or driving in the car or lying in bed. Our brains are out of gear. One of us ambushes the other with a question: What was the name of that hotel we stayed in last time in New York? Who stars in *Three Men and a Baby?* What kind of a bush did we have in the front yard of our last house? Do you remember our Minneapolis phone number?

The one rule is that the person asking the question must know the answer and be able to supply it when the other person becomes desperate and whines that he or she can't rest without the answer.

Once in a while at night, when the lights are out and one of us is dozing off, the other will whisper in the darkness, "What was the name of that green and red Christmas plant?"

There's always a chance the other one's lost it again.

In Good Company!

MIKE GIESBRECHT

$\mathscr{R}$ecently I went to my local Family History library to do some genealogical research. The room I was in, its walls lined with bookshelves, was small and taken up almost completely by a big study table.

Every place at the table was occupied by a researcher, not one of them under sixty. There was barely room enough to breathe in that small room, much less to move around. Out of courtesy to others, everyone was being as quiet as possible.

After a while the door opened and a very ancient, frail little lady appeared. She was a volunteer worker at the library, and she was dragging behind her a step-ladder, which was taller than she was. Several people at the table moved to help her but she waved them off, indicating that she could manage.

Then five or ten minutes passed while she laboriously wrestled with the ladder, moving it inch by inch past the table, bumping the chairs and knocking stuff off on the floor. The atmosphere was getting somewhat tense in the room, but not a word was spoken. A few glances were exchanged around the table, I think in wordless agreement that we would not insult her by indicating the job was too big for her, considering her age and physical condition.

Finally, she was able to maneuver the ladder clear to the opposite side of the room, where she heaved a quiet sigh and gave the ladder a little shake to test its steadiness. Then slowly, step by rickety step, she began to ascend the ladder, while everyone in the room held his or her breath in wary expectation. At last, she reached the top of the ladder. She paused for a moment, then looked down and said in a puzzled voice, "Now what in the world did I come up here for?"

It brought down the house.

Lost Election

EDGAR A. GUEST

A merchant in a small town ran for office and was overwhelmingly defeated. He polled so few votes that he appeared ridiculous in the eyes of his neighbors, and both his social and business standing were in danger. It's hard to be laughed at and still hold your ground.

But this merchant was a good sport. What is more, he knew the perils of becoming the town joke. So he beat the town to it! The morning after the election he put this sign in his window: "$25 reward for the name of the man who cast that vote for me."

Everybody saw it, and everybody laughed. But they laughed with him and not at him. People came into his store to shake hands and congratulate him on his sense of humor and sportsmanship. The story of the sign went the rounds of the county, and farmers began to drop into his store to trade. Thus the merchant turned defeat into a personal triumph by proving that he was the town's best loser.

Jailhouse Prayer

JACK R. CHRISTIANSON

*T*wo young brothers were arrested one Saturday night for vandalizing an old vacant home. The arresting officer knew they were not bad boys but wanted to scare them a little in hopes that he might teach them a valuable lesson in their young lives. He took them to jail in handcuffs, booked them, and fingerprinted them. After this rough treatment, the boys were terrified and had vowed in their hearts never to do anything wrong again.

The officer was quite pleased with his teaching. When he felt that he had taught the lesson well enough, he phoned the boys' father, explained everything, and asked him to come and pick up the boys. Their father responded with a question: "Can you legally keep them in jail for twenty-four hours?"

"Well, sure," responded the officer. "But they've learned their lesson and are ready to go home now."

The father interjected, "If you can keep them in jail for twenty-four hours, I would like you to do so."

"But, sir. You don't understand. I've already scared

them to death, and I'm sure you won't have a problem with them in the future."

Emphatically the father insisted: "If you can legally keep them, I want them to stay!"

"Sir?" the officer asked. "Aren't you a Mormon?"

"Yes," was the reply.

"Don't you want your boys in church tomorrow morning?"

"No! I want them in jail so they can really learn a lesson."

The officer couldn't believe it, and neither could the two brothers.

The next morning when the officer took them breakfast, he stopped and listened as they discussed their dad having left them in jail all night long.

"I can't believe it!" the oldest boy muttered. "He left us all night!"

"Yeah," responded the younger of the two. "I've never felt bad about missing church until someone told me I couldn't go."

Looking at his watch, the oldest said, "We've already missed priesthood meeting, and Sunday School will start in five minutes."

The younger brother then came up with a grand idea: "Why don't we have our own Sunday School. I'll pray if you'll give us a lesson."

The older brother agreed. The officer continued to watch and listen, still holding their plates of food. Then the younger brother began to pray the only way he knew how: "Dear Heavenly Father. We're so grateful that we could all be here today. We're grateful for this beautiful building we have to meet in." And then the kicker. "Please bless all those that aren't with us this week, that they will be with us next week!"

Brother Perfect

PAT FAIRBANKS

When my oldest son was a junior in high school he was asked to be the youth speaker in our sacrament meeting. His topic: Repentance.

As he began his talk he said, "To illustrate that we all need repentance, if there is anyone in this room who has never committed a sin, will he or she please stand up."

Just then, the somewhat hard-of-hearing ward clerk, who was seated at his desk on the podium, stood to begin his descent into the congregation to count the attendance.

Immediately realizing that his entire talk was at risk, my son turned his head and gaped at the clerk. As the congregation burst into laughter, the poor clerk checked his tie, checked his fly, and then just looked at the congregation and shrugged his shoulders and went on about his business.

The talk continued as planned, but throughout the meeting there were sporadic bursts of muffled laughter in the chapel, and the shoulders of the members of the bishopric were seen bobbing up and down as they tried to contain their mirth.

Of course the ward clerk was later informed of the reason for the laughter and has since that day, more than twelve years ago, been good-naturedly referred to as "Brother Perfect."

To Sing or Not to Sing!

ROBERT BEAN

As a member of the Air Force I was under-going some training at Fort Leonard Wood, Missouri, an army training base for heavy equipment operators. One day in church our small congregation, consisting of one Airman, one Marine, and about 30 Army soldiers, was struggling through a hymn when we sang the words ". . . And Jesus listening can hear/The songs I cannot sing" (*Hymns,* no. 227). Whereupon we all stopped, looked at each other, and then started laughing! I'm sure we were not the only ones laughing at our singing!

Love and Laughter

The Case for the Tried and True

JOSEPH WALKER

*I*t was going to be the prom dinner to end all prom dinners. And to tell you the truth, we were pretty proud of ourselves for coming up with the idea.

"Who wants to go to the same boring old restaurants everyone else is going to?" I asked. "We want to come up with something new. Innovative. Creative. Different."

"Well," Danny joked, "we could always get Kentucky Fried Chicken."

"Yeah, right," I said. "Like we're really going to walk into the Colonel's wearing our tuxes and formals to pick up a bucket of chicken. The girls would never talk to us again."

"What if we didn't eat there?" Jim wondered. "What if we took it to someplace fancy?"

"Come on, Jim," I said. "Fancy restaurants won't let you bring your own food in."

"Then what if we set up a table someplace else—like a park or something?"

"That'd be great!" Ernie proclaimed. "That way the

girls would be so impressed with our creativity that they wouldn't notice how cheap we are!"

The next few minutes got a little crazy with all of the wild, off-the-wall, nonboring ideas flying around. Eventually, we decided to rent a U-Haul truck, set up an elaborate dinner table in the back, and spend a romantic evening motoring around town while we ate. The way we saw it, it would be like having a picnic in a gondola while floating through Venice. Only without the water. Or the boat. Or the scenery.

On prom night we brought our dates to the parking lot where the truck had been set up. The girls were perplexed until we ceremoniously opened the back door. It was an incredible sight, if I do say so myself. Our hefty table was covered with a linen tablecloth, and the china, crystal, and silver were perfectly arranged. It was as nice as any restaurant, and the girls were properly impressed by our originality as we escorted them to their places.

If only we could have stopped right there. But no, Jim had to go and close the door.

"Real funny, guys," Linda said, giggling in the dark. "Now, somebody turn on a light."

A light? What a great idea! Too bad none of us had thought of it earlier.

"Please, Joe," Colleen said. "I don't care if lights are boring. It's too dark in here."

"Kurt," I said hopefully, "did you see where the light switch is in here?"

There was only silence. A very long, very painful silence.

"Come on," Linda said, the giggle gone. "You guys aren't that dumb, are you?"

I wanted to smack Linda for calling us dumb. But I couldn't see her in the dark.

"Wait," Danny said. "Jim has a flashlight . . ." His voice was overwhelmed by the sound of the truck engine starting. He tried the door, but it was locked. He made his way to the front and pounded on the wall. Jim shifted into gear and the truck lurched forward.

"Let me guess," Colleen said, coolly. "You can't communicate with Jim, can you?"

It was at about this time that Jim hit the first speed bump. A couple of crystal goblets shattered on the floor of the truck. One of the girls screamed. Then Jim took the first corner. The whole table started sliding. Everyone else screamed. I could just see tomorrow's headline: "Eight Students Crushed to Death in Fried Chicken Fiasco!"

An hour later Jim finally opened the door on what looked like a war zone. Seven goblets were in pieces on the floor, mingling shards with twelve china plates of various sizes. One chair leg was broken, and one female ankle was sprained (an ugly incident with mashed potatoes and gravy). My date's dress had been smeared by a flying bucket of fried chicken.

"Mmm-mmm," I joked feebly. "That perfume you're wearing is finger lickin' good!"

It didn't help. The dress was ruined. And so was the evening.

A few weeks later, when we were finally able to laugh at ourselves again, Jim voiced a suspicion that we had all been considering. "Maybe," he said, "the boring way of doing things has been around so long because . . . well, because boring works."

I've been thinking about that lately as I've tried to keep pace with all of the creative solutions being offered for age-old problems. And while I'm all for creativity, it seems to me that those who are suggesting that traditional moral standards have become outdated are forgetting one important fact: they are traditional because they work. There may be more innovative ways of doing business or developing relationships, but none is more effective than the tried and true. Honesty is still the best policy. A penny saved is still a penny earned. Integrity is still a value to be cherished. Virtue is still better than vice.

And not because it's boring, but because it works.

Love and Basketball

DOUGLAS COLTON PERRY

*L*iving with my wife, Janice, and her talents has always been interesting. Before I met her, she was already a fine musician and a great athlete. I guess, if the truth were told, she probably should have become a professional athlete—she was just born thirty years too soon. I'm sure she could have quarterbacked her high school football team and taken them to the state championship—she's that good.

So, between her music and her other talents, sports occupy a lot of her life. During the 1998 NCAA finals, she was flipping channels, watching the University of Utah Utes play in the championship series and the Utah Jazz play on another channel. I came into the room and needed to know something.

"Honey," I said, and asked her the question. She didn't respond—she was still changing channels.

"Honey?" Still no response.

I said, "Jani, do you love me?" Still no answer.

I shook her shoulder gently and finally got through. "Hmm?" she said.

I asked again, "Do you love me more than basket-ball?"

Without looking up she said, "College or pro?"

My First Kiss

LISA MANGUM

I was what was known as a drama groupie in high school. All my friends were in the drama class, but since I was so shy, I did the next best thing—I became the class aide. It was a cushy job—occasionally grading papers, periodically running errands for our young, single drama teacher, Steve, and mostly hanging out with my friends while they were supposed to be "rehearsing."

Every fall the high school performed a musical, and during my senior year we performed *Once Upon a Mattress*. My two best friends landed roles in the musical; I asked Steve, our drama teacher, if there was anything I could do to help out behind the scenes. He put me to work on a variety of jobs, including taking roll at each after-school rehearsal. I would stand by the door and check off everyone's name as they came onstage. I got to know everyone, including the fifty or so people in the chorus. I loved being a part of the play without actually having to perform.

That is, until about three weeks into rehearsal when I

was suddenly and unexpectedly called upon to . . . perform.

I was standing by the door, checking the roll, and talking to my best friend, Valerie. Off to the side of the stage, a couple of actors were running through their lines, practicing a scene that involved a stage kiss. But the girl kept laughing right before the kiss. Pretty soon, Steve came over to dispense some drama-teacherly wisdom.

"The problem," he said, "is that you're thinking too hard about it. It's not a real kiss—it's just a stage kiss. Here, watch!"

I looked up just in time to see Valerie bolt like a frightened rabbit off the stage. The next thing I knew, Steve took hold of my face and kissed me soundly on the lips.

Steve turned to the cast and said, "See? It doesn't mean anything." Without another word he picked up his script and notes and headed back to the drama room.

I just stood there—the roll in one hand, my pencil poised midair in the other. Valerie cautiously crept back to me and asked, "Are you okay?"

Dazed, I replied, "Steve just kissed me. But it didn't mean anything." I looked at her and we both started to laugh.

Making the "D'wight" Choice

DWIGHT DURRANT

$\mathcal{M}$arci and I were in the same ward at BYU. One Sunday, after I had participated in passing the sacrament, I noticed an empty seat next to her. I had seen her around, but I didn't know her name. I asked permission to take the seat, and while the talks were being introduced, I decided to use a line on her right there in sacrament meeting. Now I know some of you are thinking that it's not appropriate to use pick-up lines in church, but I would like to remind you that one of the highest ordinances of the gospel is temple marriage.

So I turned to her and said, "Don't you owe me dinner?" What a dumb line. She didn't even know my name. Of course she didn't owe me dinner, but she felt so sorry for me that she agreed. I said, "How about right after sacrament meeting?" She said okay.

When we got to her apartment, to her embarrassment, we were not able to find any food in her cupboards. I felt bad, so I said, "My parents live just a couple of blocks from here. They always have food at their house and they are at church right now. If we hurry, we can go get some of their food before they get home."

We raided my parents' kitchen, then went back to Marci's apartment to fix dinner there. After dinner, we spent the rest of the day together. Finally, at about 9:30 P.M., I decided I had better go. But before leaving, I asked Marci for a date. She accepted, and we had so much fun on the first date that I asked her out again and then again. It was like a new world record for me. I started to think that maybe I had found the right one.

However, there was a problem: Marci already had a boyfriend. Nevertheless, I decided that she was worth going after. When I asked her out, she would always say yes, and we would have a great time together. But it seemed that wherever I went, I would see her with this other guy. I had grown to like her a lot, and seeing her with another guy was very frustrating to me. I couldn't stand the thought of her having another boyfriend. I think this is called "two-timing."

Finally, I decided I couldn't take the pain any longer. I told her she had to make up her mind—that it was going to be either him or me. She promised that she would decide soon. It was shortly after giving her this ultimatum that we were sitting together waiting for sacrament meeting to begin. I asked her if she had made up her mind, and she responded that she had not. It was then that a miracle happened.

The organist began playing the introduction to the opening hymn. This hymn has since become my favorite. Of all the hymns that could have been chosen that day, the one that we began to sing was "Choose the

Right." Hey, I'm no dummy. I picked up on it right away and began to sing extra loud. I needed to send her a message because, obviously, I was the right choice.

I kept glancing at her, but it wasn't really working. She didn't appear to be feeling the inspiration. As the second verse was being sung, I was inspired to change the words just a little. Instead of singing "choose the right," my first name being Dwight, I began to sing at the top of my voice: "Choose D'wight, choose D'wight." I guess it worked because she soon told the other guy she had made "D'wight" choice. Marci and I have been together ever since.

A Wish

IMPROVEMENT ERA

They were at a picnic. "You see," he explained, as he showed her the wishbone of a chicken at the luncheon, "you take hold here and I'll take hold here. Then we must both wish a wish and pull, and, when it breaks, the one who has the bigger part of it will have his or her wish gratified."

"But I don't know what to wish for," she protested.

"Oh, you can think of something," he said.

"No, I can't," she replied, "I can't think of anything I want very much."

"Well, I'll wish for you!" he exclaimed.

"Will you really?" she asked.

"Yes."

"Well, then there's no use fussing with the old wishbone," she interrupted, with a glad smile. "You can have me!"

Baking Bread

DOUGLAS COLTON PERRY

$\mathcal{S}$oon after we were married, Janice and I moved to Pacific Grove, California. I was in the army and studying Russian at the Army Language School at the Presidio of Monterey. We lived in a tiny, cracker-box home. Our bedroom was our living room and dressing room with a curtain across part of it to hide our clothes. We had a bathroom, a tiny kitchen, and a front and back door. Every day, new bride Janice worked to perfect her cooking skills, and each day she'd ask me, "Honey, what would you like for supper?"

One day I suggested she bake some homemade bread. My mother had taught me how to make bread, so I wrote down the recipe for Janice and left for school. All day I thought about coming home to aromatic, delicious homemade bread.

When I entered the kitchen door that evening I smelled nothing. No wonderful aroma. I went down the hall to the living room/dressing room/bedroom and found Janice crying on the bed. She just pointed to the kitchen. I walked back to the kitchen and noticed what

I hadn't seen the first time. There on the counter were two brand-new, glistening aluminum loaf pans, and way down in the bottom lay this *dead bread.*

I picked up one of the loaf pans and discovered that the pan itself had been basted both inside and out. It slipped out of my hands and thunked onto the kitchen floor.

"Did you forget to cool the scalded milk before you put the yeast in?" I called to Janice. I was sure I had told her.

Then I laughed—a big mistake. The bedsprings squeaked, and I heard footsteps coming. I'm smart, though, and I nipped out the kitchen door. She bounded down the hall, scooped up that wad of dough, and from the doorway threw it at me. I was somewhere between the azaleas and the rhododendrons, but with her arm and aim, that dough smacked me on the back of my head.

When I regained consciousness, I was face down with my head near a rosebush. I could hear her in the kitchen fumbling with the other loaf tin. I knew my life was in danger, so I quickly rolled over and in self-defense grabbed the first dough wad, lying there covered with grass, leaves, and dirt. Her second lob missed me, and I threw the first wad back at her. Then we threw these big, gooey globs of dough back and forth. At first she was trying to kill me, and I was just trying to survive. But as we continued to hurl them at each other, the globs hit in midair and coalesced. After that, we'd throw it, and it would elongate in the air and wrap itself around us as it landed. We started to laugh, and before long we were laughing so hard we couldn't even stand up.

So it was we learned that joy can come after pain. I had a headache for three days, but Janice eventually did learn to bake good bread.

We're All in This Together

Quieting the Chaos

SCOTT HIXSON

*O*ne day my father came home from work eager to have a relaxing evening. When he walked in the door he was greeted by the chaotic noise of children recently home from school, letting out pent-up energy. In an attempt to calm our home, he asked my sister, Shauna, to go tell all the neighbor kids they'd have to go home. Shauna quickly obeyed, but came back a few minutes later and said, "Sorry, Dad, they're all ours!"

Don't Nuke Those Squirrels!

JOSEPH WALKER

$\mathcal{I}$t sounds sort of trivial, now that I think about it. But for some reason, it seemed like a big deal at the time.

The issue was pants. *Joe's* pants. Not that he wasn't wearing them (which really *would* have been something to get worked up about). It's just that he was wearing them . . . well . . . wrong.

"But everybody wears their pants like this, Dad," my then-eleven-year-old son protested, his trousers hanging so low on his hips that they barely covered what they were intended to cover. "It's *cool!*"

"Yeah. Cool," I replied. "And it'll be downright chilly if you ever bend over."

"But, Dad . . ."

"Look, why don't you just pull them up . . . to here," I said, helpfully hiking his trousers up to where it had been "cool" to wear them when I was in high school. I cinched his belt tight around his waist. "See—that feels much better, doesn't it?"

"It feels like I'm being cut in half," he said, sourly.

Then he glanced in a mirror—and grimaced. "Oh, great. Now I look like a nerd."

Knowing that the only thing worse than actually being a nerd is looking like one, I tried to make light of the situation. "If anyone accuses you of being a nerd, just show them your last report card," I assured him. "Anyway, that's why God gave you a belly button—so you'd know how high to wear your pants."

Joe didn't think it was funny. "Hey," he said, "just because you use your belt to help you suck in your stomach doesn't mean I have to—"

"Hold it just one minute. Are you saying that I'm fat?"

"Are you saying that you're not?"

"Well . . . so's your old man!"

"*You're* my old man!"

"Oh, yeah?"

"Yeah!"

I went to Anita for some moral support, and all I got was laughter.

"You've got to be kidding," she said, still chuckling. "Can't you guys find anything important to argue about?"

"Important? Anita, we're talking about the boy's pants here!"

"I understand that," she replied patiently. "What I don't understand is—what's the problem? If he likes to wear his pants lower than you would, so what?"

I mumbled something about how deteriorating dress standards had led to the decline of the Roman Empire, the Boxer Rebellion, and Cher, but deep inside I knew she had a point. Or, at least, that I didn't have one. The fact is, it *doesn't* matter that Joe wears his pants lower than I would. And maybe, by making an issue out of it, I risk winning a battle with my son while losing precious ground in the ongoing war for his trust and love.

I guess we all do that from time to time. We make big deals out of little deals simply because we're unwilling to accept someone else's right to think for themselves. We start drawing lines in the sand, and before we know it, we've boxed ourselves into defending positions that are ultimately indefensible because they boil down to subjective judgment—my opinion against yours.

Which is not to say that we should avoid taking a stand on potentially divisive issues. There are some positions that are worth defending, no matter the cost. But you've got to pick your battles—and your weapons— carefully. Like a friend of mine says, "You don't need nuclear bombs when you're huntin' squirrel."

Of course, sometimes in the heat of battle it's difficult to tell whether the heavy artillery should be hauled out or locked up. The pants issue is—I'm embarrassed to say—a pretty easy call when it comes right down to it. But what about those other issues that come up in families? Tough ones, like when you say eleven o'clock is a reasonable curfew for your sixteen-year-old, and she thinks all curfews are ridiculous. Or when your twelve-year-old decides he wants to have his nose pierced. Or when your spouse thinks you really need another credit card—just for emergencies—and you're sure that one more credit card will topple the delicate balance of your checkbook. Forever.

Sorry, but I can't help with specifics. You're going to have to work them out on your own, case by case. All I can say is be careful. Pick your battles. Don't draw lines in the sand you aren't ready to defend.

And remember, don't nuke those squirrels!

Unconventional Dinner

LORI BOYER

*M*y brother-in-law is a master at turning potential fiascoes into fun. When he and my sister were first married, she was nervously getting ready for her first back-to-school night as a high school history teacher. She was much closer in age to the students than to the parents. Thoughts of presenting to them her teaching plan for the year thoroughly intimidated her.

For dinner she put some chicken pot pies in the oven. When her husband came home from work, she asked him to listen for the timer, get the pies out, and call her in from the other room where she would be getting dressed. After a bit, she heard the creak of the oven door, followed by a crash and resounding clatter. Already tense, she snapped, "That better not have been the pot pies!"

When there was no answer from the kitchen, she assumed Jim had knocked a pan off the counter or dropped a lid or something. She returned to mental rehearsals and distracted hair combings. When Jim called, she headed to the kitchen. On the floor in front of the oven was a modest mound of chicken pot pies. Surrounding the pies on the floor were place mats, silverware, and Jim, looking eager to eat. Not only did she laugh, but she joined him on the floor and went off to back-to-school night fortified by chicken pot pie à la linoleum and the thought that, really, very few things in life are worth getting uptight over.

Do You Remember When?

JOSEPH WALKER

*I*t was supposed to be an intimate, romantic dinner for two. Anita had planned it as a surprise for me and spent the biggest part of the afternoon preparing a gourmet feast: shrimp cocktail, lemon chicken with lemon-dill rice pilaf, baby carrots in butter sauce, and my favorite, cherry cheesecake for dessert.

She set up a card table for us in our living room. For that evening, however, it became *Chez Walker,* complete with a linen tablecloth (okay, so it was really a bedsheet; but in the candlelight it *looked* like a linen tablecloth), china, our best silverware, and the soundtrack to *Somewhere in Time* playing on the stereo.

The way Anita had it planned, Joe and Andrea would take care of their little sister and brother in the kitchen while Amy served as our maître d'. But then Joe remembered a Scout camp he was supposed to attend. Amy's afternoon baby-sitting job continued well into the evening, with no end in sight. And Andrea had come down with the flu.

So *Chez Walker* became a restaurant-nursery-hospital

ward. Andrea was sprawled on the sofa to my right, intermittently drifting in and out of nausea. Elizabeth occupied the high chair to my left, expressing herself artistically with a rice and carrot floor mural that will forever be remembered as *Il Fresco d'Uncle Ben et Bugs Bunny*. And Jonathan was plopped in my lap because . . . well, that's where he wanted to be, and you know how insistent a five-month-old can be about such things—romance notwithstanding.

The evening's most memorable moment occurred between the shrimp cocktail and the main course, with Andrea hunched over the garbage can, trying to decide whether or not to throw up; Elizabeth announcing that she needed to be changed; and Jon letting it be known—pungently—that he likewise required diaper maintenance.

Dim the lights. Soften the focus. Cue Cole Porter: "Isn't it romantic? . . ."

To say that the evening didn't turn out exactly the way Anita planned is a little like saying the economy isn't exactly doing as well as the president hoped it would. But do you know what? The dinner was still delicious, the company was still first-rate, and we probably laughed a lot more (during and since) than we would have if we had gone out to the most expensive restaurant in town. We made a memory—one that will last a lifetime. Years from now it will probably be recalled with happy smiles, tender hearts, and the words, "Do you remember when . . . ?"

I hear that phrase a lot whenever I get together with my dad and my older brothers and sisters. And I'm impressed by how often it's the difficult times that are recalled. Sure, we remember when we went to Disneyland. But there is so much more joy in retelling the story of how, during the waning days of the Great Depression, Mom sent Dad to work with what he thought was a salt and pepper sandwich, when it was really just her way of sending seasoning for his hard-boiled eggs. (His coworkers felt so sorry for the poor man who could only afford a boiled egg and a salt and pepper sandwich for lunch that they took up a collection for him. Dad thought it was funny. Mom was mortified.)

Then there were the family experiences during World War II while Dad was stationed at Pearl Harbor and Mom was stationed at home. We still can't decide who of the two faced the more hazardous duty—Dad in harm's way in the war or Mom at home with five children under seven years of age.

And then there were the years of economic struggle for our large family, during which time brothers Dick and Bob tried to teach little sister Wanda about the dangers of smoking by having her suck on one end of a piece of rolled cardboard while they applied a match to the other end. Drawing the raw flame into her mouth, Wanda learned her lesson, all right: steer clear of Dick and Bob.

Examine your own family history. You'll probably find similar memories anchored in troubled waters. It says a lot about the resiliency of the human spirit that so many of our most treasured recollections are inspired by adversity. Perhaps that's because character is shaped more by the things that go wrong than it is by the things that go right, and the way we confront life's challenges will, to a great degree, determine our success on this planet. We remember how we deal with difficulty because it has so much to do with who we are and what we eventually become.

Which is not to say we should go out looking for hard times. Believe me, they will find us. But maybe we shouldn't fear them so much. When adversity comes—as it inevitably will—think of it as a memory under construction. Such thinking may not make the crisis any easier to handle. But at least it will give you something to look forward to—even if it's only being able to look back and say, "Do you remember when . . . ?"

The Little Plumbers

CHRIS CROWE

I've had my share of crazy days, but one from several years ago remains etched in my mind like a kid's handprint on a newly poured patio. In those days, Christy and Jonathan liked to team up for fun and mischief while I read the paper and Liz was busy making dinner. Christy was four, Jonathan was two, so she called the shots.

That evening's shots were being called from the bathroom, where the two little plumbers had locked themselves to splash, play, and generally enjoy a little kid's life without any annoying interruptions from Liz or me.

An ominous silence (all silences in a house with two kids under five are ominous)—followed by a series of toilet flushes, giggles, and gurgles—alerted Liz and me to the scene. When we crashed their indoor beach party, the kids, the floor, and the walls were drenched with toilet water. Jonathan's yellow bathtub boat bobbed in the gentle tide of the toilet bowl, while the two little culprits, dripping with wide-eyed innocence, tried to explain what had happened.

Liz and I had been in the parenting game long enough not to be fooled by a couple of cherubic looks; the overwhelming circumstantial evidence condemned them on the spot. We disinfected them, spanked them, and sent them outside to safer and drier activities. The evening wore on, as evenings do; the bathroom returned to normal; and we forgot about the incident.

Later that night when I revisited the damp disaster area, it was obvious that somebody (or somebodies) hadn't been flushing the toilet. I didn't think much of it—after all, an unflushed toilet isn't all that unusual in a house inhabited by a four-year-old—and gave the toilet handle a yank.

The tank gurgled, the bowl bubbled, but instead of whirling everything neatly down the toilet drain, the murky water rose over the lip of the bowl, splashed onto the floor and over my bare feet.

I hopped from one foot to the other, yelling for Liz. When she came to the bathroom door, she looked at me sitting on the bathroom counter, my feet dripping wet; at the mess on the floor; and at the steady stream of water spilling over the edge of the toilet bowl.

"Toilet's clogged," she said.

As she stood in the safety of the hallway, I sat on the sink, and together we watched until the water ceased its relentless sludge over the edge of the toilet bowl.

To make a long, grimy story short, the plumber's friend, coat hanger, and Playtex-gloved hand (guess whose hand?) couldn't unplug our toilet again. I knew that on the morrow I would have two unpleasant alternatives: call a plumber and blow a chunk of our savings in one grand flush, or attack the problem myself with screwdriver, wrench, and my bare hands.

I decided to tackle it myself. If it was simple I'd be able to do the job and save the cost of a plumber. If it was complicated, I was sure to make it worse, guaranteeing that the plumber would earn his pay.

Later that evening around bedtime, as I was contemplating the day's disaster, Christy walked through my room on her way to use our toilet. On her way back to her room, I asked her about the flooding, hoping to discover what I'd be up against in the next day's amateur plumber hour.

"Christy," I said, "'member when you and Jonathan were playing in the bathroom today?"

She didn't answer. Even a four-year-old knows better than to incriminate herself.

"C'mon," I wheedled, "you're not in trouble now. Do you remember when you two were playing in the toilet?"

She nodded.

"Did you put anything in there besides the boat?"

"Nope," she answered cautiously. "We were just washing it."

"So you didn't put anything else in there? No toys? No dolls? No shoes?"

"No, Daddy. We were just washing the boat."

"Did you use washcloths?"

"Just two."

"Which two?"

"The ones from the hall closet."

"What happened to them?"

"But, Daddy, we were just using them to wash the boat . . . one is still okay. I put it back in the closet."

"Still wet?"

"Uh-huh."

"Great." (Job's patience kicks in about here.) "What about the other washcloth?" I asked, anticipating the awful answer.

"It drownded."

Mystery of the Missing Coat

EMILY BENNETT WATTS

*W*hen my children were little, sometimes they would get hopping mad. If you've had a toddler, you've probably seen that little face screwed up and ready to burst into tears in frustration. In our house, when a child is in that state, we usually say, "Don't laugh." Because their emotions are so close to the surface anyway, it's easy to switch them over to the laugh track. Sometimes you have to say it two or three times: "Don't laugh . . . ah-ah-ah, I see a laugh coming . . . oh-oh, here it comes!" They try hard to keep frowning, but pretty soon they laugh. Whatever they were mad about has been forgotten.

I remember once being extremely frustrated with my two-year-old daughter. I don't remember now what she had done, but I do remember her looking up at me with her big, green eyes and saying, "Don't laugh, Mom." It worked! I couldn't be mad at her anymore; I couldn't be frustrated. It was a moment of perspective for me.

A similar moment came when I was serving as Relief

Society president in my ward (in itself a cause of humor for some). I was pregnant and had a big maternity coat. This was a large coat. This coat could have served as our family's emergency preparedness tent. One homemaking night, I hung my coat on the rack in the ward house— and it got stolen. I was perplexed. Why on earth would anybody steal what was obviously not a highly fashionable coat?

When I got home and poured out my sad tale, my husband pointed out that a person could shoplift half of Albertson's under that coat—a twenty-five-pound turkey could have been hidden in its folds, and nobody would have noticed. Somehow, that knowledge failed to make me feel better. Whatever the reason for the theft, I had no maternity-size coat. I was upset, and being pregnant, I cried a lot more than I cry normally.

Observing this, my two-year-old son got a very determined look and volunteered, "I will get mad at them for you, Mom." The thought of my small son going out to battle the hooligans who had filched my coat settled me down enough to restore some perspective. This loss was not the end of the world. I didn't want that coat anyway—and after the baby was born, I wasn't going to wear it again ever—so it was all right. That mountain shrank back down to its proper molehill size.

Practicing for Christmas

RICHARD MOORE

I love Christmas. I always have. Memories of past Christmases flood my mind each year as I listen to familiar carols, wrap packages, and smell the aroma of the tree.

In our family, each Christmas had a uniqueness to it that we use to recall that particular day. It's not, "Do you remember Christmas in 1967?" Instead, we say things like, "Remember the Christmas when our neighbor's roof caught fire?" or "the Christmas when Grandpa sang on my new tape recorder?"

Several of my most vivid memories of Christmas as a kid revolve around the theme of "practicing for Christmas." It began one year early in December when my parents had gone shopping and left us kids home. As they drove out of sight my older sister said to me, "We need to practice for Christmas."

"What do you mean?"

She explained, "Every year we ask Dad what time we can get up Christmas morning, and every year the same thing happens. He asks us what time we want to get up

86

and we say four o'clock. He tells us we are not getting up at four, but that we can get up at eight o'clock. We tell him we get up earlier than eight o'clock every day and then ask him if four-thirty is okay. He says NO WAY, but moves the time we can get up to seven o'clock. We argue that seven is too late. How about five? This goes on until we settle for six o'clock."

I don't see her point, so I ask, "What are we going to practice?"

"Well, if we are so quiet that we don't wake anyone it won't matter what time we get up."

This concept seemed awfully sneaky and maybe even dishonest. I liked it. She explained what she wanted to do and the practicing began. I would go down to my bedroom in the basement, lie on my bed, and pretend to be asleep. She would go to her room and get on her bed. Then, she would get up and go through the hall past my parents' bedroom, through the kitchen, and down the stairs to my room. She would touch my arm and say very quietly, "It's time." I would then get up without saying a word and follow her through the basement, up the stairs, through the kitchen, and into the living room where we had flashlights hidden so we wouldn't have to turn on the lights.

My sister would then say something like, "That went pretty well, but you hit two or three creaks on the stairs and another one in the kitchen—let's do it again."

Back I would go to the basement and we would repeat the whole process. We practiced every opportunity we had when our parents left the house.

By Christmas Eve I knew we were ready. At bedtime

we hugged and kissed Mom and Dad goodnight and started to go to our rooms. Dad said, "Hey, aren't you going to ask what time you can get up tomorrow morning?"

"Six o'clock, right?" my sister said.

"Six would be fine, but aren't you going to argue that you need to get up earlier?" My dad was clearly surprised.

"Six o'clock is okay with us, huh?" I said, giving my sister that knowing look. She returned a knock-it-off-you-dweeb-or-you'll-tip-them-off look. In a voice that clearly sounded as if we had simply resigned ourselves to their dictates she said, "I guess six o'clock is fine. [sigh] Goodnight."

Some may not understand why getting up early on Christmas is so important. This is likely because you bought into a family tradition that everyone should have breakfast together first and then enter the living room as a family at about 8:30. Clearly, you simply don't know any better. It's just the way you were raised. The truth is: if you are not up *before* six o'clock on Christmas morning, you have missed Christmas. I know, I know— you still have most of the day left, but let me tell you, "kid Christmas" happens early. The earlier the better. If you can open every present, play with your new stuff, and be bored before 5:30, you have experienced a real kid Christmas.

Excited about the possibility of a great kid Christmas, I said my prayers, hopped into bed, and began the grueling task of trying to fall asleep. Here on earth we normally function on regular time. But once a year on

Christmas Eve, for just a few hours, time reverts to heaven-time where one day equals a thousand years. Many people do not know this because they are asleep and everything seems normal to them. For you people who sleep through it—trust me, Christmas Eve is a time anomaly.

I lay in bed that Christmas Eve not able to sleep. I looked at my glow-in-the-dark watch: 11:20 P.M. I determined that looking at the watch too often made time go even more slowly and decided not to look at the watch for at least one hour. Two and one half hours later I looked at the watch: 11:42 P.M. Aaaaaagh! This cannot be! I waited a full four hours this time before looking at my watch: 12:17 A.M. Three weeks later it was 2:05 A.M. . . . Then, it was morning. Morning? I looked at the watch that didn't need to glow in the sunlight: 8:32 A.M. I had missed Christmas!

I rushed up the stairs to find the entire family up and in by the tree, even Dad. "Hey, sleepyhead, I thought you were going to get up at six."

"Why didn't somebody wake me?"

Mom answered, "We figured if you could sleep in on Christmas morning, you must need the sleep."

I looked at my presents from Santa under the tree and opened some other packages from family members. I got *what* I wanted, but I didn't get them *when* I wanted.

When no one else was around I confronted Sharon. "Why didn't we get up early like we practiced?"

"I've been up since twenty after four," she said. "I was going to come and get you, but decided that I couldn't trust you to be quiet enough so we wouldn't get caught. You were just too big a risk. Maybe next year you'll be ready."

I thought about telling my parents what she had done, but then decided that would ruin my chances for next year.

The next year: My older sister didn't say anything about practicing for Christmas during the first week of December. When my parents went shopping the second week and she didn't say anything, I approached her.

"Aren't we going to practice for Christmas?"

"Practice for Christmas? That's for kids. I always thought that idea you came up with was stupid anyway."

She had gotten older, and practicing for Christmas had become not only a stupid idea, but *my* stupid idea. "Okay," I replied, trying to let her know that I had no problem with dumping the whole plan.

I then went straight to my little sister, Janean, and said, "We need to practice for Christmas, and I'm going to show you how." I explained everything clearly. I even gave her a copy of a map I had made showing the location of every floor creak and groan in the house. Waiting until both my parents and Sharon were out of the house, we practiced whenever we could. After our final practice I looked Janean straight in the eye and told her, "No matter what happens, I'll be coming for you. You can trust me. I won't leave you behind."

A valuable hint for all Christmas practicers: Waking a person who is pretending to be asleep during a practice session and waking a person who really is asleep on Christmas morning are very different things. When it was time, I gently shook her and whispered, "Janean."

Nothing. I shook her again and whispered a little louder, "It's time." Still nothing. Why wouldn't she wake up? I decided to go for broke. I shook her hard enough to make the bed rock and said as loud as I dared, "Hey, wake up!" What happened next shocked my entire being. A weaker heart would have failed.

My little sister, Janean, had awakened about midnight with the stomach flu and had thrown up quite a few times over the next couple of hours. My parents had stayed up to take care of her until about 2:30. Finally, Mom decided that the best thing to do was to have my little sister come to sleep in our parents' bed where Mom could keep an eye on her and help her if she got sick again. Figuring that Dad needed the rest, Mom insisted that Dad go sleep in Janean's bed. The trade was made, but I was not informed.

Yes, I woke my dad at 3:24 on Christmas morning. He shot straight up in bed and barked, "What? What's wrong?" I believe it was the only time in my life that I screamed like a girl. I think I hit a note that only dogs can hear. Terror gripped my soul and rational thought fled. I considered swaying back and forth with my arms above my head chanting, "It's a dream, it's a dream," but thought better of it.

"Where's Janean?" I asked.

"She's in bed with your mother. She's sick. What time is it?"

"I'm not sure," I said. I wasn't positive. It could have been 3:25 or 3:26 by then.

Dad looked at his glow-in-the-dark watch. "It's not

even three-thirty!" Stupid watch. "You get back in bed and don't you dare get up until six!"

I flew back to bed, not even trying to avoid the creaks. That was the last year I ever practiced for Christmas.

Peace on Earth

SCOTT HIXSON

My Dad is famous for getting engrossed in reading the newspaper. One evening he sat in his chair reading when my sister, Shauna, tried to get his attention.

"Dad?" she said.

No reply.

I tried to help out. "Dad!"

No reply.

Then my brother, Craig, joined in. "Dad!"

Finally, all three of us combined to attempt to break through. "DAD!" we yelled.

That's when he had had enough. He abruptly brought down the newspaper and pleaded, "Will you kids stop fighting!"

Santa Claus Calling

RICHARD MOORE

One distinct memory I have of Christmas is going through the toy catalogs to decide what to put on my wish list. I was always very careful not to ask for too much. I remember being aware that no matter what Santa brought, my parents had to pay for the items and so I had to be reasonable in my requests. We didn't have a lot of money. One year I had my heart set on a present that I believed was more than my parents could afford. So, I compromised and asked for only one walkie-talkie! Now, I never claimed to be a really bright child, but I do feel a need to explain. My cousin, Jeff, lived about a block away. We figured that if we each asked for one walkie-talkie we had a better chance of getting them than if we each asked for a set. Besides, he was the only guy I was going to talk to anyway.

On Christmas morning that year I got up earlier than I was supposed to. There was the walkie-talkie under the tree. I picked it up, clicked the "on" switch, and heard the exciting sound of static. "Calling Jeff, calling Jeff," I spoke into the walkie-talkie while pressing the button for speaking. No reply. Again, "Calling Jeff, calling Jeff." Still no reply. A third time: "Calling Jeff. Calling Jeff." When I lifted my thumb from the button, a voice came from the speaker that was definitely NOT Jeff. "Richard," a deep man's voice came clearly from the walkie-talkie. "Richard, go into your parents' room."

Fear gripped my soul. "It's Santa Claus," I announced to my little sister. Her eyes got wide.

"What does he want?" she asked.

"He wants me to go to Dad and Mom's room."

"Why?"

"Because we got up earlier than we were supposed to and now he's making us confess to Dad and Mom. I'm afraid Santa is going to make me give my walkie-talkie back!"

"What are you going to do?"

"I'm going to go wake them up and tell them the truth; you can't not do what Santa says—you might not get any more presents for the rest of your life!"

I made my way through the dark kitchen and into the hallway to my parents' door. I rapped lightly on the door, not sure that I really wanted to go through with this.

"Come in," I heard my dad say.

When I opened the door, the light was already on, and I saw my dad sitting up in bed holding a walkie-talkie. I don't remember seeing my dad more excited on Christmas morning than that day. "What took you so long to get up?" he asked me. Later, my mom told me that Dad couldn't sleep that night because he wanted to be sure he was awake when I got up. He kept saying, "What is keeping this kid? He should be up by now."

Go figure.

Grandpa's Greatest Shot

LISA MANGUM

*F*amily traditions. Every family has at least one. Maybe it's something seasonal like decorating the Christmas tree together, or lighting fireworks on the Fourth of July. Perhaps it is something outdoors: camping, fishing, or a yearly trip to the mountains to see the autumn leaves. I like to think that in addition to the rather "traditional" traditions, every family has at least one tradition that is unique.

In my family, it's throwing napkins after dinner. Specifically, it's throwing napkins *at Mom* after dinner. I don't remember how the tradition started, but my best memories of family dinner always end the same: Dad crumples up his napkin, leans back, and lobs it across the length of the table at Mom. Mom shrieks, laughs, and tries to defend her empty glass with her hands. My brother cries, "Goal tending!" and heaves his napkin into the air. More often than not, Mom throws Dad's napkin back at him. And more often than not, he volleys it right back at her in the same motion. I knew my future husband would fit right in when one night at dinner he tossed a napkin that bounced off my glass and straight into Mom's.

For many years my brother held the record for the best shot—a clean hook that sailed right over the dining room light fixture and landed in Mom's water glass. Swoosh! Nothing but splash!

His record stood until Grandpa came to town for a visit. Dinner was winding down and pretty soon the napkins started flying. Eventually Mom was laughing so hard she had to call a time-out to take a drink of water. And then it happened. From out of nowhere came the bank shot off Mom's nose and into her glass—mid-drink. The crowd went wild. We all turned to see who had made the spectacular throw. There was Grandpa, sitting quietly at the end of the table, a twinkle in his eye, and his napkin conspicuously absent from his plate.

$90 Apricots

HEATHER PACK

My friend called and said that they had two apricot trees and just couldn't keep up with the hundreds of ripe apricots. She wondered if I wanted some. Since this was my first summer in Utah, I thought it might help me assimilate into the culture by bottling apricots. I thought *How hard can it be to bottle apricots? Plus, they're FREE!*

My adventure began with opening up my trusty cookbook, *Better Homes and Gardens*. It had never failed me in the past, so I knew I could rely on it to teach me how to bottle fruit.

The directions seemed simple enough: boil the apricots for twenty seconds; peel off the skin; put the apricot halves in bottles; add syrup and steam the bottles for thirty minutes. What the directions failed to mention is that the process requires three out of the four burners on your stove, both sections of your kitchen sink, and every pot you have in your home to complete this task. My whole kitchen was under siege!

The last piece of advice the cookbook gave was to

keep your work surface clean and to work quickly. Reading that now causes me to break into hysterical laughter.

The first thing I realized is that twenty seconds is not long enough to cook the skins off the apricots. After three to four tries I realized it takes at least a minute. But this also partially cooks the apricot. So much for cold-pack canning.

The directions also said to place the apricots face down in the bottle. I had no idea how I was supposed to do that. I just dropped the apricot halves in and hoped for the best. So much for face-down apricots.

After pouring in the syrup, I was supposed to place a nonmetallic spatula in the jar to get out all the air bubbles, a procedure that causes the sticky syrup to spill all over the jar and the counter. So much for my clean work area.

I had started the project at 10:00 A.M. I finally finished steaming six quarts of apricots at 11:15 P.M. So much for working quickly.

As I pulled the jars from the steam canner I discovered the syrup was pouring out of the jars. The directions had said not to *over*tighten the lids. What it failed to mention is that they do need to be tight, however. So much for my ½-inch of headspace.

I gave up and went to bed.

The next morning with renewed vigor I decided to give it another try. I called my husband to see what he thought I should do with my first six quarts. "Call my mom and ask her," he said. What my husband didn't realize is that meant calling my mother-in-law and admitting that her darling son had married a woman who didn't know the first thing about canning. So much for my image of being a competent wife. Finally, at noon I was steaming my second set of jars. I began to think . . . just how *free* has this adventure been?

I made a list:

Parts

Steam canner	$34.50
Canning funnel	1.99
Canning jar lifter	3.95
10 1-quart glass jars	2.40
Jar rings	2.49
Jar lids	1.99
10 cups sugar	1.89
Labor, 14 hours, 10.00 per hour	140.00

(Actually, I feel I'm worth much more than that, but I'm offering a discount summer rate.)

Damages

Lunch at McDonald's	$13.02

(There was no way I was making lunch . . . no room either.)

Rental of a carpet cleaner for both the kitchen and the front room	$40.00

(My 2-year-old decided to "help" by peeling and pitting fresh apricots on the floor in both the kitchen and front room.)

Manicure, to get rid of my orange-stained cuticles	$25.00

(Okay, I admit, I didn't get the manicure, but I sure deserved one!)

I realize that it isn't fair to include the price of the

steamer, funnel, and jar lifter in the cost because they can be used over and over again. But I can promise you I have no intentions of using these items over and over again! I subtracted the number of jars that didn't seal, which was seven. So my three remaining jars of apricots come to $89.08 each. I think at the store you can buy a can of apricots for $1.09.

The funniest thing of all was, I wasn't even sure if my family *liked* canned apricots! That winter I found out.

They don't.

Missing Death Date

MARY ELLEN EDMUNDS

$\mathcal{A}$ few weeks after my father passed away, I was picking up the mail at the post office and noticed an official-looking letter addressed to "Friends and Family of Ella M. Edmunds." Wow—that seemed like a message to survivors. Why would there be a letter like this when Mom was still with us, when it was *Dad* who had gone Home?

I was very curious, so I went directly to Mom's place and showed it to her. We opened the letter, and she had me read it to her. It began, "Friends and Family of ELLA M. EDMUNDS . . . We were recently notified of the death of ELLA M. EDMUNDS. . . ."

It was one of those moments when just about anything could have happened, including bursting into tears (my feelings were still so tender about Dad being gone) or even getting angry that such a stupid mistake could have been made.

But what did happen was typical for our family. I looked at Mom and asked, with great drama, "Why didn't you *tell* us?"

The letter went on to say that "the exact date of death was not given. Please enter the date of death in the space provided below and return this letter to us."

My brother Frank suggested that we have a kind of lottery—each of us could put in $100 and make a guess as to when the date might be. Winner take all. He told Mom she could even be included if she'd like, and if she got it right we'd split her winnings among the rest of us. Oh, my. To some this may seem an inappropriate or even irreverent approach to things, but it works for our family now and has for many years.

Families Are Forever . . . Is That Some Kind of Threat?

Lecture #3

LORI BOYER

As a parent of eight, I find myself repeating lectures so often even I get bored with them. Often my kids are bored, too. In fact, they even have numbers for the lectures. When I begin the discourse on the dangers of leaving backpacks by the door so that a mother trips over them, they have been known to nudge each other and say, "Here goes lecture number 6." Sometimes my lectures are so memorable they can even recite them with me. I try to convince them that I give the same lectures day after day because things just don't get done. But sometimes a fresh approach gets the point across better. For example, one night at dinner everyone had forgotten their table manners. Eight hungry, grabby, gabby children proved oblivious to lecture number 3 on what napkins and silverware are for and number 11 on transporting food without injuring others at the table. By the end of the meal my husband and I knew we had to try a new tactic. The next night, dinner began as usual, but as soon as he heard the amen on the blessing, my husband yelled, "Lori, the casserole!"

I scooped out a huge blob of casserole and catapulted it down to Richard's end of the table with an overhand shot. About one-third landed on his plate, one-third on his lap, and one-third on the dog's head. Richard immediately frisbeed a tortilla to my end of the table and then dived ravenously into the Mexicali casserole on his lap. I, meantime, was shoveling food into my mouth as fast as I could and elbowing everyone around me. The children froze in horror. Then they started laughing. It was the funniest lecture they had ever seen.

Too Many Kids—
Not Enough Drugs

BRAD WILCOX

$\mathscr{S}$usan and Joe Shumway, with their family of six small children, had been vacationing in Mexico. Joe's work required him to return to their home in Laramie, Wyoming, a few days early, and Susan, pregnant with number seven, found herself shepherding her brood through customs and having to deal with mounting distractions and problems.

"There I was," she recalls, "out of money and out of diapers. I was trying to keep track of all the luggage and all the children at the same time. I was so pregnant I could hardly walk." The man at the customs counter looked from Susan to her six noisy charges and back to Susan. "Lady, go right on through," he invited. "If you have drugs in those bags, you need them."

I Love My Dad

RANDAL WRIGHT

Mike Anderson, a fellow CES employee, related this experience he had with his young son.

In the early 1970s my Church Educational System assignment required me to travel a great deal. In order to keep in touch with my children, I would often take one of them with me in my travels. On once such occasion my six-year-old, Mike, and I traveled from Springfield, Missouri, to Fort Smith, Arkansas. As we drove along the Interstate, I asked him about school and related topics and then decided it would be a good time to teach my son something about the creation of life.

To determine the level of his understanding, I said, "Mike, have you noticed there is a difference between boys and girls?" After thinking about it for a moment, he said, "Yes, Dad. Girls are pretty and boys are ugly!"

Though I was tempted to chuckle, I remained serious and tended to somewhat agree with him. I asked if he realized what it meant for his mother to be pregnant.

"It means she is going to have another baby!" he said.

"Well, son, do you have any questions about that?"

He thought for a moment then asked, "Does everything Mom eats go down and hit the baby on top of the head?"

Again, I had to restrain my impulse to laugh. I explained that the baby was carried in a special place, so that the food did not hit him in the head.

For the next forty-five minutes we had a most interesting talk as we traveled toward our destination. Finally, as the conversation waned, I told my son how much I had enjoyed our talk together. Then wanting to recap our experience, I said, "Mike, what did you learn from our discussion today?" I was anxious to hear him repeat some of the great knowledge I had imparted to him. He pondered for some time, then stood up in the seat of our old Volkswagen. He stepped over the console, put his arm around my neck and said, "I learned I love my Dad!"

IRS-2K Form, No Kidding

TERRI WINDER

$\mathscr{I}$'ve just finished filling out my income tax return, but something seems amiss. My figures don't honestly reflect the year's financial picture. Somewhere in between the Standard Deductions on the 1040 and Itemized Expenses on the Schedule A, there should be an optional 2K form, short for "two-year-old kid." That form should read something like this:

2K Credits

How many outfits does your two-year-old wear on an average day?

How many of those are permanently stained?

Subtract line 2 from line 1. Enter results here.

How many times does your child remove his shoes and socks each day?

How many pairs of shoes have been outgrown but still look brand new?

Multiply the amount on line 5 by 5 and subtract from line 4. Enter results here.

Measure the square footage of the area your child can cover while sitting at the dining room table. If your floor

112

is vinyl, multiply this amount by 10%. If you are dumb enough to have carpet you get a 20% deduction, providing you use your tax return to help pay for new vinyl. If you regularly serve oatmeal for breakfast, you may take an additional 15% deduction. Spaghettio's for lunch qualifies you for a one-time 20% deduction, plus one educational credit.

List miscellaneous expenses here. These may include—but are not limited to—Ruined Items (i.e. lipstick, sunglasses, wallpaper, broken dishes).Wasted Items: (i.e. toothpaste, shampoo, cold cereal, spilled milk).

NOTE: If you were able to salvage any part of Wasted Items (for instance, the toilet tissue that was pulled off the roll) subtract that amount before entering total.

Enter the replacement amount of any permanently damaged appliances under Major Expenses. Examples are: jammed toaster (any flavor of jam qualifies); dishwashers with doors that have been stood on; and broken lamps. NOTE: If anything larger than your automobile has been destroyed, you must attach a separate sheet of explanation.

Add together the above amount with lines 3, 6, 7, and 8, and enter here.

Do you have a nanny or governess? If not, multiply the total by 4. If you take your child to daycare, subtract the total amount by one half.

This is your deductible amount. Enter here and on Form 1040, line 36B.

I'm sure it is just an oversight that this form doesn't already exist. Perhaps all it would take is a suggestion.

Parents of two-year-olds should write their Congress-men and the IRS. (The real possibility that the two-year-olds might be grown by the time the proposal becomes law should not be a deterrent). In the meantime, parents of two-year-olds should just take a double child credit.

Most people perceive the IRS as being inhuman and unable to compromise, but I think they'd be reasonable about this. After all, some of them are bound to be the parents of two-year-olds themselves.

You Tell Me

EILEEN R. YEAGER

*W*e were visiting another ward. This was before the "block" program, and sacrament meetings were an hour and a half in length. Sometimes longer.

My husband and I had struggled to keep our six children—ages infant to eleven years old—occupied and reverent. There were the usual disruptions: bathroom breaks, drinking fountain runs, and quarrels, but all in all, we thought we had done a pretty good job.

The meeting finally came to an end, and we began the process of gathering our things while trying to keep the children together. As I worked I noticed that an older couple seated directly behind us had not moved, and in fact seemed to be waiting for something.

When I paused, the wife looked directly into my eyes, and in a soft voice, tinged with real concern said, "I have a daughter who lives in Arizona. She has six young children. I was just wondering . . . how is she?"

Bath Time for Bozos

JANENE BAADSGAARD

*P*arents everywhere have a special before-bath dirt gauge to tell them how much fun their kids run through during the day:

One sticky child = Just a little bit of fun, but nothing to brag about.

One smudgy child = A little bit more fun than a little bit, but still nothing to write to Aunt Mabel about.

One dirty-elbows, dirty-knees child = A good-time-was-had-by-all-fun.

One dirty-all-over child = Fun and I mean the brag-about-it, write-it-in-your-secret-journal kind.

One no-skin-showing child = A lot more fun than plain ordinary brag-about-fun—the kind that gives parents gray hair.

One smoldering child = So much fun the child dazedly brags about it to the guys in white coats in the emergency room.

Parents everywhere stand in the doorways of bathrooms, raise their washcloths, and declare, "Give me

116

your tired, your poor . . . your dirty masses, so I can breathe free."

Children exhibit such paranoid tendencies when it comes to taking a bath. With newborns, you generally have a small tight bundle who screams bloody murder whenever you try to gently unravel him enough to get him undressed and into the water.

This delightful process progresses to the next developmental stage where the child doesn't even have to see water before he starts undressing himself. At this stage, you will sometimes find your child out in the front yard dancing in the nude. Don't be alarmed. This stage will pass.

Childhood bath-time paranoia next progresses to a rather pleasant stage of sudden water love. The only drawback to this stage is you often have difficulty finding your child under all the trucks, dolls, wozzles and wazzles he drags into the tub with him. This same child regularly refuses to get out of the tub and get dressed, even when his skin looks like an aging prune.

Enjoy this stage, it doesn't last long. Before you know it, you have a child who doesn't want to go near the bathroom unless he's desperate for something other than the tub. This sudden dislike of bathing seems to last forever. You send the child to the "Tub," and 3.5 seconds later, the child dashes out with peanut butter still smeared on his cheeks, black dirt lurking in his toenails, and hair that looks like you threw him in the drier without a static-control sheet.

Just when you're sure the Board of Health is coming to pick up this child for disease control, he suddenly comes down with an adolescent addiction to the little room with a lock on the door. You will not see your child for years unless you call him to pizza or the telephone. You'll swear your daughter's curling iron will permanently weld to her head and your son's wet towels on the bathroom floor will start growing mushrooms.

Surely there must be an easier way to keep your children clean. Maybe an in-home water slide is the answer. I never have any trouble getting the kids excited about someone else's water.

Joseph Fielding Receives a Whipping

JOSEPH FIELDING SMITH

$\mathcal{I}$t wasn't much of a whipping. . . . [My father] did it because he thought I had lied to him. He didn't do it because I had done something wrong, but because he thought I hadn't told him the truth. And so he gave me a cut or two across the back. Years afterward I said to him one day, "Do you remember when you gave me a lashing?" and told him the circumstances, "because you thought I had told you an untruth?"

"Now," he said, "I don't know that I remember a thing like that."

"Well," I said, "it happened. . . ."

"Oh, well," he said, "we'll let that apply on something you did when you didn't get caught."

Excuses, Excuses

LYNN C. JAYNES

$\mathscr{L}$evi is trying to decide if he needs to stay home from school or not today. This presents a real dilemma, as he has to wrestle with which absentee notice to turn into the school principal when he returns. I keep several signed notes in my drawer, and he gets to take his pick and fill in the blank with his name. These are his choices:

Note #1:

"_____ had a doctor's appointment this morning because he is a pain—I mean he had a pain. The doctor said he's not dead, yet. Please excuse him from classes, although he says he wouldn't mind making up the recess."

Note #2:

"Please **do not** excuse _____ from school today. He deserves every 'zero' you give him. He woke up cranky and hating everything from the breakfast pancakes to the toothpaste. He couldn't find a clean shirt except for the ones on his floor that he's been stepping on for two days, and he forgot to do the assignment in history due to a late night, very intense episode of "I Love Lucy." I have sent him back to his room with a list of nasty chores for the day. He should be done by about 2:00 this afternoon. Would you like me to send him to you then? I guarantee that by then, he will be miserable and hating staying home plenty; I should think you'd look pretty good to him."

Note #3:

"Dear Teacher, You did not have the pleasure of my son's disposition in class yesterday, and for that you can thank me. I gave him permission to go hunting. I know this is generally not an excused absence, but hear me out: He ardently desired to feel like a mighty meat-gatherer, and I've been living with that macho attitude for over two weeks now. We have two choices here— you can give him zeros on missed assignments (to which he will respond, 'Mighty hunters don't care about little goose eggs'), or we could let his blistered feet, sore leg muscles, empty game bag, and the flat tire he had to change be their own punishment. The bonus to us both is that his primal chest-beating and yodeling are now much subdued. I think we both won."

Note #4:

"Dear School: I have been working through my list of people to send stinky notes to today, and 'you is one!'
_____ is not in class today because he informs me there is another child sitting behind him in class who constantly picks at him and says disgusting things to him. I've tried to teach my children that we don't pick noses, we don't pick mothers, and we certainly don't pick at other kids. And, if we don't pick, then we can

expect the same treatment from others. Now please, Teacher, I may be a whiny mother, but don't make me out a liar too."

Note #5:

"Dear School, Yesterday _____ spent the day at home down-loading. He did not have enough RAM to continue operating at a competitive level, and his monitor was looking a little hazy. I think he caught a virus."

Note #6:

"Dear School, Someone at your fine institution mentioned at the beginning of the year that attendance at a funeral constituted an excusable absence. _____ is taking you at your word and now reads the obituaries faithfully. Providence has been in his favor of late, and, as you know, he has had several opportunities to mourn. Though we must excuse his absence today, with a little forbearance, I think we can break him of this. From now on, do not excuse him unless he can at least spell the name of the deceased."

Note #7:

"Dear Teacher, There is no excuse for my child's ditching school today, but my mother-in-law lives out of state—let's blame her. You can send _____ home the minute you get him straightened out.

P.S. I won't expect him for supper."

As you can see, Levi has quite a problem figuring out which one to take this morning, if he misses school. But these are his only choices; I've spent many hours writing them, carefully choosing which words to use and signing each one. They are in my drawer, at the disposal of my children, whenever they decide to miss school.

I can rest fairly sure the kids are smart enough to real-ize just how much damage their mother can do.

And mom wins again.

Overflowing Bathtub

LINDA J. EYRE

$\mathcal{O}$n a Mother's Day morning, as I was running the bathwater for my two- and three-year-olds, I decided that they needed to practice some songs for the Mother's Day program at church later that morning. The songbook, however, had been left in the car the night before.

I'll just quickly slip out to the car and get it, I thought as I scampered across the kitchen, still in my old white nightgown, and stepped into the garage. The door from the house into the garage closed behind me. I could hear fifteen-month-old Josh, who had followed me as far as the door, complaining about being left inside. He fiddled with the doorknob as I rummaged through the car for the songbook. After a couple of minutes of searching through suitcases, dirty clothes, and empty Styrofoam hamburger boxes, I laid my hands on the songbook and went running back to the door, only to bash my nose as my momentum was stopped with a bang.

With horror, I realized that the baby's fascination for pushing buttons had carried through to the doorknob, and that I was locked out. I could hear him still shuffling around in the hall, but no matter what I said, he just couldn't figure out how to turn that knob without at least one lesson from someone on the same side of the door.

Dying at the thought of running around our well-exposed house in my "lovely" nightgown, I had almost decided to wait until Daddy would get home from his meeting in about half an hour, then I remembered that I had left our two little girls in the bathtub—with the water running!

Swallowing my pride, I took a long breath and tiptoed swiftly out of the garage door, around the house, and climbed onto the balcony and to the bathroom window, which had the kind of glass you can't see through. For some reason, it seemed that if I tiptoed, people wouldn't see me. I could hear the water running full blast and the children's voices.

"Saren," I called gingerly to our oldest daughter (the three-year-old), trying not to speak loudly enough to call any attention to my presence from the neighbors. No response. The running water was too loud. "Saren," I yelled, louder and louder until it reached an almost scream. At last she recognized my voice.

"Mommy!" she shouted. "It's getting hot!" *Just what I wanted to hear!* I knew she didn't know how to work the knobs on the tub. In horror all I could think to say was, "Get out of the tub."

"I can't hear you," she kept saying through the thick, frosted window.

Casting all modesty to the wind, I yelled louder and

louder: "Get out of the tub. *Get out of the tub!* GET—OUT—OF—THE—TUB!"

I could feel the neighbors' kitchen curtains parting behind me, but I didn't look around and wave. I just clutched my nightgown, which the breeze was whipping around me, a little tighter and yelled, *"Come and open the balcony door!"*

After several more "I can't hear you's" from Saren and shouted instructions on my part, she finally padded over to the sliding glass door. I had heard two-year-old Shawni giggling about all the commotion, so I knew she wasn't in distress—yet. Only a few more seconds and I would be able to pull her out of the rising water.

As Saren reached the door in her birthday suit, dripping from head to toe, I began to explain how to open the door and realized that my trial was not yet over. That door was almost always unlocked, so she had never tried to open the lock on it before. Pushing the lever in the right spot was a fairly complex maneuver for a three-year-old.

I tried to remain calm and explained over and over just how to open the door. After what seemed like an eternity, she at last hit the right spot and, in a flash, the door was wide open. I threw out my arms and picked up Saren on my way into the bathroom, where we found Shawni shoulder deep in water, enjoying her toy boat bobbing at almost nose level, with the water pouring down the overflow valve. The baby toddled in to see what all the commotion was. It would be years before he would realize what a riotous Mother's Day story his penchant for pushing buttons had produced.

Locked in the Bathroom

CHRIS CROWE

$\mathcal{O}$ne Sunday, shortly after we had moved to Japan, proved to be especially memorable.

"Daddy, potty!" Carrie announced to everyone within shouting distance of us in sacrament meeting. "Daddy! Potty!" she repeated more loudly, guaranteeing we'd make our exit with an audience.

Normally I didn't begrudge two-year-old Carrie her sacrament meeting potty trips, but on that particular Sunday I was scheduled to be the last speaker on the program. Liz was out of the chapel feeding Joanne, so I took Carrie and hoped I'd make it back in time for my talk.

In the bathroom, I nudged her toward the toilet stall and turned to comb my hair. I had just pulled out my comb when I heard a "click" behind me.

It wasn't your average door-closing click; it was an ominous, uh-oh, toilet-stall-locking kind of click that reminds you to never let a two-year-old do anything alone, especially in a bathroom minutes before you're supposed to speak in sacrament meeting.

As soon as it clicked, I knew there was going to be trouble.

"Carrie," I called through the door, "it's time to come out, honey." In reply she shoved her panties under the door.

"Carrie, listen to Daddy. We've got to go back to church. Open the door, okay?" A hard knot of anxiety began forming in my stomach. My daughter's trapped in this toilet stall, I have a talk to give in a few minutes, and my Japanese translator's sitting alone on the stand with a copy of my talk in hand probably wondering if I had already been translated or had just chickened out at the last minute.

"Carrie, unlock the door, please. I want to go to church." I heard her tugging on the lock.

"Daddy . . . Daddy! Want out," Carrie cried, realizing her predicament.

I couldn't reach over the door, and she couldn't crawl under it. Carrie would have to open it herself, or I'd have to figure out some way to open it for her.

"Hang on, Carrie, I'll be right back," I called to her as I left the bathroom in search of a ladder or footstool.

I grabbed a chair from the Relief Society room and carried it back into the bathroom. Carrie grinned when she saw me looking down at her over the top of the stall. "Hi, Daddy. Stuck." She pointed to the door.

"I know, babe. Unlock the door, 'kay? Push on that knob. That's it. No, the other way. 'Atta girl. No, push harder." She couldn't budge it, and even from my perch atop the chair, I couldn't reach it.

It's funny how your mind works at times like these. I

128

should have been worrying about getting my daughter safely out of the toilet stall, about giving my sacrament meeting talk, about avoiding the huge potential for embarrassment that would permanently taint my family in this face-saving country if sacrament meeting were interrupted by the arrival of a phalanx of firefighters to rescue my female child from a toilet stall in the men's restroom of the only LDS church in a city of half a million. But I couldn't help laughing to myself.

With the sounds of the beginnings of a Carrie tantrum echoing behind me, I hustled back to the Relief Society room and went through the closets looking for a broom or a pointer or anything long enough to reach the door's latch. Nothing. Next I tried the kitchen. The longest thing I could find was a large, lacquered serving tray. It'd have to do.

When Carrie saw me back at my perch, she interrupted her tantrum long enough to kick the locked door a few times and to add a few more layers of toilet paper to the mound she had shredded while I was gone.

"It's okay, Carrie. I'll get you out." I lowered the serving tray—it wasn't quite long enough to reach the latch, so I stood tiptoe on the chair, one leg out for balance, and leaned over the top, teetering on my stomach as I hung headfirst down into the stall.

After a few swings of the tray, I connected, and the door popped open.

I hopped off the chair and handed Carrie her panties. "Put these back on, and I'll be right back." Hoping I still had time for my talk, I grabbed the chair and serving tray to return them.

On my way out the bathroom door, I ran into Sister Daimon and her three-year-old son in the hallway. "Konnichi wa" ("Good afternoon") I said as I smiled and hustled past her, the chair in one hand and the serving tray in the other. I didn't have the time or the Japanese to explain what I was doing with a Relief Society chair and serving tray in the bathroom.

Slightly rumpled and trailing shreds of toilet paper as we went, Carrie and I made it back to the chapel just in time to have the bishop introduce me as the last speaker.

Out of the
Mouths of Babes

101 to 97

RANDAL WRIGHT

$\mathcal{O}$ur family loves basketball. During a tight play-off series involving my favorite professional team, I was disappointed to be involved in taking care of a household chore during a critical point in the game. Seeing that Nichelle, our eight-year-old daughter, was not busy, I asked if she would mind going downstairs to check the score of the game. She said okay and after a few minutes came back up and reported that the score was 101 to 97. I was really proud of her for being so responsible. I waited for her to tell me who was winning, but it became obvious that she had nothing else to say. Finally I said, "Nichelle, which team is winning?" She looked at me very strangely and said, "Duh, Dad, the team with 101 points."

"Good Job, Dad!"

VIRGINIA U. JENSEN

*M*y oldest child, a daughter, got married just three weeks before her husband started medical school. Thirteen years later, he finished his medical training. In those long years of hard work, there were some deficiencies in their life. One was the amount of time they as a family had with Dad. Soon after my son-in-law began his practice as a neuro-radiologist, he was asked to lecture to an auditorium full of doctors at a noon seminar. It happened to fall on a much-needed day off. In response to the request, my son-in-law said, "I have promised my four-year-old daughter, Elizabeth, that I will spend the day with her. If I can bring her along to the lecture, I will do it." The agreement was made; Mom fixed a lunch for Elizabeth to eat during Dad's speech. With Dad at the podium, Elizabeth sat quietly on the front row between a couple of doctors and ate her lunch. As Dad left the podium to return to his seat at the conclusion of his presentation, Elizabeth exclaimed in a voice that could be heard on the back row, "Good job, Dad!" The audience exploded in laughter.

Super Bowl Winners?

MELODY MALONE

$\mathscr{S}$everal years ago I was sitting at the kitchen table with my four little girls discussing the upcoming Super Bowl. We were expressing our desires for who we wanted to win and why and who we thought would win and why. When, with as much enthusiasm as a five-year-old could muster, my daughter said, "I want the Boyd K. Packers to win!"

Tone of Voice

RANDAL WRIGHT

*S*everal years ago my six-year-old cousin Casey was playing her first year of girl's softball. During the first game, she got a hit and ended up on third base. When the next batter came up and hit the ball, Casey made no effort to run toward home plate. She just stood on base as if nothing had happened. Seeing this, the coach desperately tried to get her to run for home plate, so she would score. He began yelling loudly, "Go home, Casey! Go home!" He called to her several times, each time louder, but Casey remained on third base. He looked on in disbelief when Casey finally bolted in tears from third base to her mother in the stands. After her mother got her calmed down, she asked Casey what had upset her so much. Casey replied, "The coach told me to go home!" By the tone of his voice, she hadn't understood that he meant home plate.

"Yea! He's Dead!"
MARNI HALL

*S*everal years ago our family was reading from the Book of Mormon and got to the place in 1 Nephi 16 where Ishmael dies. As we read on, my sister Karin, who was about five years old at the time, interrupted and asked, "Why was everyone happy when Ishmael died?" The rest of us were pretty confused, and we tried to explain that Ishmael's family was indeed very sad about his death. "Then why did they say 'yea'?" she asked. Sure enough, in 1 Nephi 16:35 it states, "Our father is dead; yea . . ."

Free Agency?

KERRY GRIFFIN SMITH

*S*hy children. Outgoing children. We'd seen a variety that day. Several years ago, one of the producers from the Church's Audiovisual Department and I had spent hours interviewing children to appear in a short video presentation on the Old Testament. Some of these children were represented by talent agencies and were very familiar with the interviewing process and subsequent negotiations with their agent if they got a part.

We were hoping to produce a modified LDS version of the once-popular television show "Kids Say the Darnedest Things" to add to a Church Educational System presentation. We wanted to show how much children understand, yet how different, and sometimes comical, their understanding can be from an adult's.

Throughout our interviews, we told the children Biblical stories to refresh their memories, then probed with a few questions, being careful not to prep the children for any particular responses. After telling about Adam and Eve in the Garden, we asked one boy to tell us what free agency means. He furrowed his forehead and thought for a moment before innocently replying, "I don't know about a free agency, but my agent charges."

His unexpected answer took us aback for an instant, but we couldn't contain the laughter for long. We were quite familiar with agency fees and could easily understand why the question had stumped our truthful little interviewer. Needless to say, he landed a part in the production.

Joseph Smith Was Where!

CLARIS BUTLER

We were sitting around the dining room table one Sunday afternoon discussing what we had learned in Church that day. I mentioned something that Joseph Smith had said. Our little six-year-old daughter perked up and asked, "Who said that?" "Joseph Smith," we answered, pleased that she was showing so much interest. She got an amazed look on her face and in a hushed voice stated, "I didn't know he was in our ward!"

Earplugs

CHARRI JENSEN

My mom has a hard time hearing and wears hearing aids. One day she was tending my three-year-old son, and when I picked him up from her house I asked him if he had had a fun time with Grandma. He told me NO, that he hadn't had much fun. When I asked him what had gone wrong, he told me that while watching television he kept asking her to get him a drink but that she wouldn't give him one. I explained that Grandma has a hard time hearing and that she probably hadn't heard him—that when he needed something he should go up to her and make sure she is looking at him and ask her really loud.

He looked up at me with hands on his hips and said, "Well, if she would take those stupid things out of her ears, maybe she could hear me."

Still Counting . . .

SHARON SAWYER

A few years ago, I was on a "wash your hands" kick with my kids. I told them that every time they washed their hands they had to use soap and they had to count out loud to ten. They had to count loud enough so that I could hear them, no matter where I was in the house. After several days of hearing "One, two, three . . ." the kids were kind of getting used to it.

One day before dinner, I sent them to wash up. We could hear "One, two, three . . ." from each of them as they scrubbed their hands, then they appeared, ready to eat at the table. We all sat down, and our son Travis was called on to ask the blessing. Things got very quiet, he folded his arms, bowed his head and we heard, "One, two, three . . ." His sister, Trisha, interrupted him and said, "Mom wanted you to say the blessing, not count them!"

Baptized by the Dead

DELAYNA BARR

We were having family home evening about temples, hoping that the kids were getting the message and looking forward to going to the temple someday. But our four-year-old, Maddie, was very insistent about not ever wanting to go to the temple, EVER! When we asked what she was so upset about, she said that she didn't want to go "because there were ghosts in the temple." We wondered what she meant until she explained that she didn't want to go to the temple and "be baptized BY the dead." So much for thinking that we were all on the same page.

The Voice of the Holy Ghost

TINA GUAY

I will never forget the day my niece Katreena was baptized and what she said immediately following. Just before she went into the font with her dad, the person conducting her baptism said: "Katreena, after your dad finishes the prayer, try to listen carefully for that still small voice of the Holy Ghost." It was the end of January and there was hardly any hot water for the font. After Katreena came out of the water, I went into the rest room to see if my sister needed any help. I asked Treena, "Did you hear the still small voice ?" Her reply was: "Yep. He said, 'Hurry up and get out of the water!'"

Leaders and Laughter

"Don't You Squeeze Me!"

EDWARD L. KIMBALL AND
ANDREW E. KIMBALL JR.

*O*nce, because of airplane trouble, it took [President Spencer W. Kimball] twelve hours to get home across the Great Plains. He wryly noted that he had new sympathy for the pioneers.

When an airplane hostess asked, "Would you like something to drink?" Spencer asked, "What do you have?" She mentioned coffee, tea, Coca-Cola. He shook his head, then rejoined, "Do you have any lemonade?"

"No, but I could squeeze you some." Spencer quickly said, in mock horror, "Don't you squeeze me!"

Ida's Hearing

F. BURTON HOWARD

$\mathcal{P}$resident Marion G. Romney's good-humored love for his wife, Ida, was manifested in many ways. Once he tried to get Ida to go to her doctor for a hearing checkup, but she didn't think she needed one. Convinced that there was a problem, but not being able to convince Ida, he finally decided to go see her doctor himself and consult about what should be done.

President Romney explained, "He asked me how bad it was, and I said I didn't know. He told me to go home and find out. The doctor instructed me to go into a far room and speak to her. Then I should move nearer and nearer until she does hear." In this way he could learn how bad the hearing loss was. President Romney went home to try his experiment.

"Following the doctor's instructions, I spoke to her from the bedroom while she was in the kitchen—no answer. I moved nearer and spoke again—no answer. So I went right up to the door of the kitchen and said, 'Ida, can you hear me?'"

"She responded, 'What is it, Marion? I've answered you three times.'"

"I Was in Hopes You Wouldn't Recognize Me"

FRANCIS M. GIBBONS

*P*resident Kimball's sense of humor . . . was reflected in an encounter he had with a highway patrolman. The officer saw a car driving without lights on State Street in Salt Lake City. He pulled the car over and on approaching saw that President Kimball was the driver.

"Sir," he said, "did you know you were driving with your lights off?"

"Yes," he answered, "I just noticed it."

"President Kimball," he said, "please let me see your driver's license."

"I was in hopes you wouldn't recognize me," President Kimball said.

"I was in hopes it wouldn't be you," the officer said.

Writing out only a warning ticket, he handed it to President Kimball, who said, "Now, young man, do not fail, merely because of my position in the Church, to give me a ticket if I deserve one."

Said the officer, "All right, President Kimball, if you insist."

"I don't insist," President Kimball said.

All the while this was going on, Sister Kimball sat chuckling on the passenger side of the front seat.

Japanese Courtesy

DAVID O. MCKAY

We have observed that no man (in Japan) ever gives up his seat in a streetcar to a woman, unless it be an old woman, or a woman with a baby on her back or carrying bundles. No aged person is ever permitted to stand.

The first time Brother Cannon and I were given seats, we were carrying satchels, and the kindness of the gentlemen who stood up for us made us deeply grateful. The next time, we concluded it was because we were foreigners, and were even more grateful; but about the fifth or sixth time, it suddenly dawned on me that these people were giving us seats because they thought us two old men! It seems that Brother Cannon had surmised as much before, because when I said, "Do you know, I believe I understand why these men give us their seats in the car?"

Brother Cannon smiled and said, "Has it just dawned on you?" And then for his personal comfort only, he added: "And I've noticed that you've always been the first to be given consideration."

Well, though this realization somewhat lowered my appreciation of the kindness, I still maintain that the Japanese are second to none in true courtesy and hospitality.

Brigham Young's Spelling

FROM *MEN WITH A MISSION*

$\mathcal{I}$t is interesting to contemplate Brigham Young as editor and publisher, for he was very much aware of his weaknesses, including his meager "book learning" and phonetic spelling, and recognized them with good humor. "Now my Dear Brother," he once wrote to Willard Richards, "you must forgive all my noncense and over look erours." A week later he wrote: "excuse erours and mestakes you must remember its from me." His sense of humor carried even further, as he realized that his letters to the other apostles might well be preserved for posterity. "Be careful not to lay this letter with the new testment wrightings," he told Willard Richards, for "if you doe som body will take it for a text after the Malineum a[nd] contend about it."

"Where's the Siren?"

LUCILE C. TATE

*A*s Boyd [K. Packer] began his junior year at high school he was more confident, wittier, and more fun-loving than he had been during those more sensitive years. He inherited his quick wit and sense of humor from his father.

Elder Malcolm Jeppsen tells about the triple date that he, Verl Petersen, and Boyd had with high school girl-friends. They had taken their dates home and were returning to the Packer garage to let Boyd off. At the Brigham City Tabernacle they saw Carl Josephson parked in his police car. As they passed him, Verl leaned out and gave a convincing imitation of a siren—a device that was illegal in a private car.

"Sure enough," Elder Jeppsen says, "the police car whipped around with its lights flashing and followed us to the garage, where we stopped."

"All right, fellows," Officer Josephson said, "where's the siren?"

Boyd's cool answer was: "We just took her home."

A Get-Well Wish

CARLOS E. ASAY

I, too, have experienced the healing influence of good humor. At a critical time during a recent illness, my bishop delivered a box full of cards, drawings, and messages prepared by the Primary children of my home ward. Some had tried their hand at verse; others expressed themselves in sketches and cut-outs. All were sweet remembrances that touched my heart.

A number of the greetings, however, were very funny. For example, one young lad drew a picture of me stretched out on a coffin. Protruding out of my chest was a single rose. Off to the side of the sketch were these words: "Please get well, but if not, have fun!" I laughed so loud and hard that the nurses came rushing into the room, wondering what was wrong. Those moments of humor were lifting to my spirits and, I believe, healing to my body.

Property Poem

JOSEPH FIELDING SMITH

*A*sael [Smith, grandfather of Joseph Smith] was gifted with the pen and did considerable writing in his day. He was affable in manner, possessing a quaint and genial humor and a fund of anecdote. While living in Topsfield he expressed to the selectmen of that town the amount and nature of his taxable property in this manner:—

> I have two poles tho' one is poor,
> I have three cown & want five more,
> I have not horse, But fifteen sheep;
> No more than these this year I keep,
> Stears, that's two years old, one pair,
> Two calves I have, all over hair,
> Three heffers two years old, I own
> One heffer calf that's poorly grone,
> My land is acres Eighty two
> Which search the Record youle find true,
> And this is all I have in store,
> I'll thank you if youle Tax no more.

Singing vs. Snoring

ELAINE CANNON

$\mathscr{P}$eople can solve their problems with music they've learned. You may have heard how J. Golden Kimball and Heber J. Grant solved theirs.

Heber J. Grant was an enthusiastic singer—not necessarily good, but enthusiastic. His voice carried above the congregation in the Tabernacle at general conference in Salt Lake City, Utah.

He took a trip with J. Golden Kimball once and had a bit of a problem. Brother Grant was not getting enough sleep. They were sharing a room to save money, and J. Golden snored. J. Golden was famous for snoring. J. Golden Kimball was as famous for snoring as Heber J. Grant was for singing.

Well, one night, hard-pressed for a good night's sleep, Heber J. said to J. Golden, "Brother Kimball, I have purchased some tape and I'd be much obliged if you would wear a piece of it over your mouth tonight. That way I can get some rest. I am sorry, but I am weary of your snoring."

So J. Golden Kimball, the man who snored at night,

replied to Heber J. Grant, the man who sang loudly every verse of every song in every meeting: "Certainly, Brother Grant. I'll wear this tape all night if *you will wear it all day!*"

"Fine, brother," said Heber J. Grant. "Now let's sing four verses of 'Master, the Tempest Is Raging!' before we turn in."

"But Brother Grant, there are only three verses in that hymn."

"Well, then, we'll sing the last verse twice."

Brigham's Interpretation

DANIEL HARRINGTON

There is the story told of a person who got the impression that President Brigham Young had the gift of interpreting dreams. This individual had been troubled with quite a fantastic dream throughout the night. So in the morning, he told of his exciting dream and asked President Young if he could give him an interpretation of it. The President listened to his statement. After the dreamer had finished, Brigham Young asked, "What did you have for your supper last evening, Brother Jones?" The party answered: "Well, I had quite a hearty dinner. I had some pork chops, some vegetables, and I ate half a mince pie for dessert." The President looked at him in a quizzical way, and said: "Brother Jones, you go home tonight and eat the other half of that mince pie and you'll get the interpretation."

Missionaries
and Mirth

Letter from West Africa

MARY ELLEN EDMUNDS

I receive a lot of letters from missionaries in the field. This one came from Nigeria, West Africa. It's one of many adventures experienced by Grant and Alice Gunnell.

"The only light in our house deep in the rain forest of Nigeria at 4:00 A.M. was a small glow at the end of the hall from an under-powered 40-watt light bulb. As I lay there in my bed, a black object in the hallway caught my eye. To my horror, there—only twelve feet from our bed—was the dreaded Giant Wild African Black Cockroach! Should I wake my faithful, brave husband? I decided I would attempt to rid our house of the menace myself. Each step I took I could feel the terror building inside me. It was too late to turn back now as I could see clearly his huge, three-inch body and his two fangs in the subdued light.

"During what seemed an eternity, I found my way to the kitchen. There on the shelf was the only help I could count on to rid us of this menace: RAID! As I held the can I could feel its power waiting to strike.

"Now I was only three feet away from the black nemesis of the night. My finger shook as I pressed down on the trigger. Like a cobra striking, the spray found the mark again and again. I unleashed the deadly spray until I could see the poison dripping off his two fangs. No black African wild cockroach had ever been given such a deadly, personal, one-on-one dose of RAID!

"I moved quickly to the light switch, and with one single motion I flipped on the lights. There, only six inches away from the electrical outlet, lay a dead three-inch black plug adapter, the two electric prongs dripping RAID profusely."

Tracting Woes

DENNIS GAUNT

$\mathcal{I}$t was an unusually hot day in New Zealand. The humidity was as high as the temperature, causing my shirt to stick to my back. I was on a trade-off with a "greenie," an elder who had been in the field only a month or two, and we had spent a very unproductive day tracting in a fairly affluent area in East Auckland. We were both tired, and I was getting increasingly fed up with the people in the area. Not one person had bothered to spend even thirty seconds listening to us before slamming the door shut in our faces. I was only a month or so from completing my mission, and perhaps thoughts of going home, coupled with the heat and discouragement, led to what happened.

We knocked on what must have been the ten thousandth door that day and a woman answered. I began the standard door approach and was surprised when she actually let me finish. I asked if she would be interested in hearing our message, and she politely said she wouldn't, that she had her own spiritual beliefs. I asked her if she would share some of her beliefs with us and

165

suggested that we might have some common ground. Again, she politely declined, saying that she knew we wouldn't agree on her beliefs.

I persisted a bit more, and finally she said, "Oh, all right. If you must know, I'm a renowned psychic."

Before I could stop myself, I blurted out, "Well, then, I guess you must have known we'd be coming here today."

She stared at me for a second, shocked, then slammed the door.

I turned to my companion, whose mouth was hanging open at what had just happened. I began laughing and said, "Elder, I think we're done with this street."

A Matter of Evidence

IMPROVEMENT ERA

A Methodist preacher and a "Mormon" elder were debating before a large audience in England, in the early days of the Church. The elder had closed with a testimony to the divine mission of the modern Prophet and the truth of "Mormonism." He knew, he said, that "Mormonism" was true, as well as he knew that he was addressing that congregation; and he could not know anything more positively and certainly. The minister arose and began to put objections.

"I should like to ask the elder a few questions," he began. "How does he know all this so surely? Does he know it by the evidence of sight?"

The elder said he did not.

"Do you know it by the evidence of hearing?"

"No."

"By the sense of touch?"

"No."

"By that of taste?"

"No."

"Then you know it only by the evidence of feeling?"

"Yes, sir."

"Here is a man," said the preacher, turning to the audience, "who comes to us with the statement that he knows as well as he knows anything, that 'Mormonism' is the only true church; yet when we come to inquire, his assurance is based on the testimony of only one of the five senses—that of feeling." And he went on elaborating on the "absurdity" of such a claim.

The elder knew that he must answer this in some manner, and the simpler the method, the better. So he slipped a bent pin on the minister's vacant chair and listened attentively to the rest of the argument.

At the conclusion of his speech, the preacher sat down, but rose with more speed than grace, demanding of the "Mormon" elder why he had resorted to such a childish trick.

"Why, what's the matter?" asked the elder innocently.

"What's the matter!" shouted the priest. "You know very well what the matter is. What did you put that pin on my chair for?"

"How do you know that I put a pin there? Did you see me do it? Did you hear it? Taste it? Smell it?"

"No, but I felt it!" was the retort.

The elder turned to the audience and said: "Here is a man who would have us believe that he knows that I put a pin on his chair, when he had only the evidence of a single one of the five senses!" And he dilated upon the "inadequacy" of the evidence.

A Sign-seeker Satisfied

IMPROVEMENT ERA

*W*herever the "Mormon" elder goes pro-
claiming that there is no reason why miracles should not
be performed in the Church today, he is asked, "Give us
a sign, perform a miracle, and we will believe"; and
some missionaries have a unique and effective way of
answering this ancient and absurd demand, as the
following will show:

An elder, in the early rise of the Church, was asked
for a sign by one of those bold and knowing individuals
who speak for the crowd.

"What kind of sign would be the most convincing?"
asked the missionary in a quiet and self-possessed tone.

"Oh, any physical demonstration. I'm told that old
man Thompson, when he lived here, years ago, before
we was born, had an arm put on that a machine had
pulled off. Something like that would suit us." And the
speaker took in the crowd with an incredulous grin.

"Will someone get me a large knife?"

A knife was brought.

"Now," said he, addressing the spokesman, "strip

your arm to the shoulder, and I'll perform a miracle for you."

"What'll you do?"

"Cut your arm off before this crowd, and put it back again."

"No, you won't," was the reply. And the wonder-seeker slipped away in the crowd.

Parley Outruns the Dog

DEAN HUGHES AND TOM HUGHES

We think of the early Saints, especially the early missionaries, as serious, devoted people. And they were. But they also knew how to laugh. In fact, Parley P. Pratt, one of the greatest missionaries, had a wonderful sense of humor.

Parley had been a member of the Church for only a few weeks when Joseph Smith called him to serve a mission to the "western part of the United States," in what is now Missouri. Parley took just a few days to prepare and then set out.

Parley began his mission with Oliver Cowdery, Peter Whitmer, and Ziba Peterson. But the four missionaries had traveled only about fifty miles west of Kirtland, Ohio, when they ran into trouble. Some people in the area were violently opposed to what they called "Joe Smith's Golden Bible"—the Book of Mormon. These people were willing to do almost anything to silence the Mormon preachers.

One evening Parley and Ziba Peterson were teaching a man named Simeon Carter when a police officer barged in and arrested Parley. The officer took Parley down a dark, muddy road to appear before a judge that very night. Ziba went along, too, although he was not under arrest himself.

Parley soon learned that the whole idea was to stop him from preaching. Even though the hour was late, a number of men had been brought in to make false charges. Parley decided not to defend himself against the lies. He remained absolutely silent.

The judge finally ordered Parley to pay a large fine or go to jail. Parley ignored the man. He asked Ziba to join him in singing a hymn, "O How Happy Are They."

The judge didn't think that was funny. He demanded that Parley pay the fine.

Parley had another solution. He proposed that the witnesses repent of their lies, and the judge repent of his injustice and abuse. If they would do that, and all kneel down with him, he would pray that God might forgive them of their sins.

The judge was not impressed with that offer either. He ordered a policeman, Officer Peabody, to take Parley off to jail.

The jail, however, was some miles off. For the first night, Parley was kept in a public inn. The next morning, while Parley and the police officer ate breakfast, the three other missionaries showed up. Parley whispered to them to go on without him. He would catch up soon.

He had a plan.

When Parley and the officer walked outside, Parley asked, "Mr. Peabody, are you good at a race?"

"No," the officer said, "but my big bulldog is." He

added that the dog was trained to "take any man down," on command.

Parley didn't seem to worry about that. He smiled and thanked Officer Peabody for giving him "the chance to teach and sing" and for the night's lodging—with breakfast. Then he said, "I must now go on my journey; if you are good at a race you can accompany me. I thank you for all your kindness—good day, sir."

And Parley took off running.

The officer was stunned. He didn't move.

When Parley realized he wasn't being chased, he stopped and shouted to the officer again to join him in the race. But Mr. Peabody stood amazed, seemingly stuck to the ground.

Parley turned and ran again, and this time he increased his speed to "something like that of a deer." He was two hundred yards ahead before Mr. Peabody finally remembered to send the bulldog after him.

Parley had jumped a fence and was racing across a field toward the woods when the dog finally began to catch up. Mr. Peabody was running behind, pointing and shouting, "Stu-boy, stu-boy—take him—watch—lay hold of him, I say—down with him."

The dog was almost at Parley's heels, and Parley knew that he was about to lose the race, when the thought hit him that he should "assist the officer" in sending the dog on into the forest. Parley pointed to the woods and began shouting the same commands: "Take him down, boy. Lay hold of him."

The dog flew on past and kept right on going in the direction Parley was pointing. Parley ran on, yelling loudly to the dog, and Mr. Peabody followed, farther back, shouting for the dog to turn around. But the dog had a phantom to chase, and he wouldn't give up.

Parley made it to the woods and then doubled back and slipped away. Before the day was over, he caught up with the other missionaries—with a very good story to tell.

The missionaries had a good laugh, and then they preached to a friendly audience that night. And meanwhile, Simeon Carter continued to study the Book of Mormon that the missionaries had left in his home. He became converted and traveled to Kirtland, where he was baptized and ordained an elder. When he returned home he preached the gospel and baptized nearly sixty people in the same place where Parley P. Pratt had fooled Mr. Peabody—and his dog.

They Understood Anyway
IMPROVEMENT ERA

*S*everal elders in the Pacific Islands were enjoying the luxury of an outdoor bath. Most of them were newcomers, and had therefore, just begun the use of native language with its similarities of sound and wide differences of meaning. It chanced that while they were in the midst of their plunge, three dusky maidens came along and, sitting down on the beach, began combing their hair, meanwhile viewing the spectacle of the bathing missionaries.

"*Haere mai! haere mai!*" shouted one of the new elders, gesticulating wildly.

The girls answered with a peal of laughter, and shortly afterwards began to leave.

"You'd better say *haere atu* instead of *haere mai.*"

The young man had been calling out "Come here!" for "Go away!"

A Matter of Perspective

SHAUNA GIBBY

$\mathscr{D}$uring Christmas 2001, we had two sons serving missions. Our eldest, Curtis, had been in Maracaibo, Venezuela, for about twenty months, where the year-round average temperature is around 90 degrees. Our second son, Scott, was serving in Wellington, New Zealand, and had been there for just four months.

When Curtis telephoned us on Christmas day, he said that it had been quite cold in the remote mountain town where he was serving. I asked him how cold it was, and he said that it had gotten down to 74 degrees! We laughed at that and told him he was going to be in big trouble when he came home to Utah if he thought 74 was cold.

An hour later we were talking to Scott. He had survived a cool, wet spring and said he was glad it was finally summer there. He remarked that it was hot there now. I asked him how hot it was. He exclaimed that yesterday it had been 74 degrees!

You Want What with Your Big Mac?

STEVE GILCHRIST

I was in the lunchtime line at a McDonald's in Rio de Janeiro with a companion who was, uh, Portuguese-challenged. When we reached the counter he called out his order:

"Um Big Mac, um guarana grande (one large soft drink), e uma barata frita grande (one large fried cockroach)."

When the girl at the counter looked mystified, he simply doubled the decibels: "UM BIG MAC, UM GUARANA GRANDE, E UMA BARATA FRITA GRANDE!"

I told him, in English, what he'd just ordered instead of batata frita (fried potatoes, or french fries), and gave him a quick syllable lesson on the difference between "barata" and "batata."

I then turned to the girl and said, "Acho que quero formiga cozida." (I think I'll just have some boiled ants.)

And a guarana grande.

Pray with One Eye Open

J. GOLDEN KIMBALL

$\mathcal{I}$remember when we arrived at Chattanooga, Brother Roberts sent me and a son of an apostle into Virginia. . . . When we reached our field of labor we lay around there for three weeks. I said to my companion, who was from the Brigham Young Academy, "Let us go up into the woods and see if we can sing," (I couldn't carry a tune, I never tried to sing in the Academy) "and let us go up and learn to pray." We did not have any audience, only those great big trees. And I said "Let us learn to preach." I would advise young elders to do that before they start out and not practice so much on the people; we practiced on the trees. So I prepared myself and occupied the time. My companion was prepared, and we sang. We made an awful mess of it, but after a while—and that is another testimony—God brought the tunes to us, and we could sing the songs that we had listened to in the Academy. Then I preached. God was kind to us and he loosed our tongues and we found we were able to express the things we had studied. I remember my companion was dismissing; we had our eyes shut and our hands up. I thought he would never get through; and when he said, Amen, we looked back, and there were four men standing behind us with guns on their shoulders. I said to my companion, "That is another lesson, from this time on in the South; I shall pray with one eye open."

A Holy Kiss

FROM *MEN WITH A MISSION*

*G*eorge A. Smith took the train from Preston to Manchester, where he stopped for a few days on his way to Staffordshire. There he had an experience that not only tested his sense of humor but also revealed a potential problem. Several Church members met him at the station and took him to Alice Hardman's boarding-house. Blithely unaware that the Saints in Manchester took literally Paul's biblical comments about greeting one another "with an holy kiss," he seated himself comfortably on a sofa. Almost immediately several young ladies filled the room, evidently anxious to see the only bachelor among the apostles. One of them, "decidedly a little beauty," he reported, suddenly shocked him by saying, "Brother Smith, we want a kiss of you!" while the eyes of the others flashed like "stars on a clear night."

"I never felt so foolish in my life," he wrote later, but he summoned up resolution enough to tell them that kissing was no part of his mission to England. The young women were obviously disappointed, and there-after he was regarded in Manchester as no lady's man.

When in Doubt, Don't Touch the Cat!

ABBEY ARNDT

My daughter and I were at a dinner appointment with the two full-time elders who were serving in our ward. We were at the home of a recently converted couple. After dinner we gathered in the living room, where the elders and my daughter/companion and I were to share a spiritual thought with the converts. My daughter wound up sitting on a chair next to the couple who were also sitting on chairs, while I somehow wound up sitting a little uncomfortably between the two elders on the couch. While we were visiting, the couple's cat climbed up between me and the elder sitting to my right. I was petting the cat and about ninety seconds later I realized that I was no longer petting fur but that my hand was resting on something hard . . . the elder's knee!

My face turned so red I think I nearly stopped breathing all together! I flung my hand off of his leg as soon as I realized what had happened, and in my haste I unintentionally hit the elder sitting to my left in the eye.

Everyone in the room was laughing hysterically, except for the elder with the soon-to-be black eye. The husband (recent convert—remember?) said, "Sister, I've heard of the laying on of hands, but isn't this a bit much?" Needless to say, from that point on, any elder I came in contact with was on guard just to be sure that I wouldn't either frisk him or punch him!

Shotgun and Banana

JEFF JOHNS

I was training a new elder who had only been in Germany for about a week. As we were getting into a member's car to go visit an investigator, my companion, wanting to sit in the front seat (or "shotgun"), and trying his hardest to get his point across in German, shouted, "Ich heisse Shotgun." Translation: "I am called Shotgun." The member, unfazed, simply replied, "Okay, Shotgun."

Meanwhile, back in the city . . .

That same day, his companion from the MTC was with his trainer in another section of the city, teaching a first discussion. The new elder was relating the story of Joseph Smith's First Vision. At the point in the story where Heavenly Father calls Joseph by name, instead of saying "Er nannte mich beim Namen" (he called me by name), the elder said, "Er nannte mich banana" (he called me banana).

Needless to say, at the next mission conference, everyone was excited to finally meet the dynamic duo of Shotgun and Banana.

Misunderstandings,
Mistakes,
and Merriment

Aunt Florence

MARY ELLEN EDMUNDS

*I*n our family is a wonderful soul whom we call "Aunt Florence," although I think she's actually my father's second cousin. Aunt Florence, when she was eighty-four, got a letter from a company inviting her to come and see their presentation about condominiums, telling her she'd receive a free gift—a choice between a beautiful twenty-piece set of china or a Homelite XEL chain saw. This was her response (with help from me and my mom):

"Dear Mr. Johnston: I just received your marvelous letter about the unique condominiums that you have in Park City and Hawaii. Living as I do in a nursing home, you can imagine how delighted I'd be to live in Park City or Hawaii instead. I don't know how I was lucky enough to get on your mailing list, but what a thrill!

"One thing I'm *very* excited about is the Homelite XEL chain saw. It's just what I need here at the nursing home when we work on crafts. Maybe they'll let me start coming again when they realize I've got such a nice saw; I had to quit going because I wasn't participating. I've missed it.

"Another thing I need to mention is that when you fly me over to Hawaii, I'll have to go first class. I've had several strokes, and I just can't seem to hold my knees together anymore, so I'll need the extra space.

"Thanks again for thinking of me here in the nursing home. I think that's great! Owning something 'for the rest of my life' (as you put it) sounds terrific since I'm only 84!"

Some months after Florence passed away, a letter from the IRS arrived, saying she hadn't paid her taxes for 1979. Unless she had reasonable cause for delay, she might be liable for penalties. They invited, "If you believe you had reasonable cause for filing late and for paying late, please explain. We have enclosed an envelope for your use. Thank you for your cooperation."

Well, that most certainly deserved a reply, and as our family prepared one, we could hear Florence hooting.

Under the "I did not file the form because . . ." we checked the "Business was closed" box.

In the "Remarks" section we wrote: "Yes, business was closed permanently on 9 June 1980. I'd not had an income for quite some years prior to that because I was in a nursing home. I know this is unusual to be getting a letter from me now that I'm dead, but I didn't want to mess up your records. I know how important that is to you. It was only with very special permission that I was able to send this note from the Other Side. I must say it's a lot more fun here where there aren't any taxes, but despite that I do wish you well in your work. I know a lot of people don't fully appreciate what you do, but now that I've got a new perspective (as they say) I know you work hard. By the way, in case anyone there is interested, everything they say is true—you've got to work there for what you get here, if you know what I mean. Tell the guys in the office to get with it. Thanks again for your inquiry and for providing the envelope."

Golf High Jinks

RICHARD PETERSON

*T*aking advantage of an unseasonably warm, late fall day, I slipped away from the office a little early one afternoon and drove to a nearby golf course. It was November, and at that time of the year and day the course was virtually deserted. With no one else waiting to play, I set out alone.

Knowing I had only an hour or so of daylight left, I quickly hit my drive and hurried off the tee. My second shot was a fairway wood to an elevated green. Unfortunately, I hooked the ball toward some out-of-bounds stakes to the left of the green, but from where I was standing, I couldn't tell exactly where the ball ended up.

After trudging up the hill, I spotted the ball, lying out of bounds, in the dirt in the backyard of a home that was under construction. There were two workman standing near the ball, and in an effort to excuse my errant shot, I said, "You guys ought to get hazardous pay for working so near the golf course."

"No kidding," one of them said. "This ball just hit our

buddy." He motioned toward a man who was sprawled on his back nearby.

Seeing him lying there, seemingly unconscious, I experienced a rush of fear, especially when I saw an ugly red blotch in the center of his forehead.

As I stood looking down at him, his eyes fluttered open, and he attempted to sit up.

It wasn't until he started to grin and his friends to laugh that I realized that the red glob on his forehead was a splotch of ketchup and that they were enjoying a laugh at my expense.

"You Can Just Tell"

LISA MANGUM

When my husband and I got married, my parents gave us free airline tickets to anywhere in the United States for our honeymoon. With that kind of freedom, we naturally chose to vacation in Key West, Florida—about as far away from Salt Lake City, Utah, as possible.

Of course, the downside of traveling so far away was that it took us two days to get there. By the time we drove the several hundred miles down to the Keys from Fort Lauderdale, the only exploring we were interested in was finding our hotel and then the closest restaurant for dinner. As luck would have it, we happened across a T.G.I.Friday's close by our hotel and went in.

"Just two?" the hostess asked. "Smoking or non-smoking?"

I opened my mouth to reply, but just then the waitress sailed past, plucked the menus out of the hostess's hands and said authoritatively, "Nonsmoking. Follow me."

My husband and I exchanged amused glances and followed the waitress to our table.

"It was obvious you were nonsmokers," she confided to us. "You didn't have the telltale bulge in your sleeve of a pack of cigarettes. Your teeth aren't yellow. And you don't smell of smoke." She smiled at us as we slid into our booth. "After a while, you can just tell these things." With a wink and a promise to return for our orders, she vanished into the bustle of the restaurant.

My husband and I shared a laugh over our menus before settling down to peruse our options. We were starving and it didn't take long to make our decisions.

Our waitress returned and poised her pencil over her order pad. "Would you like to start off with a drink?"

"I'd like a strawberry daiquiri," I said.

"Virgin?" asked the waitress.

The thought flashed in my mind—*That's a little personal!*—while my mouth responded rather intelligently with, "Uhm."

Our waitress looked at me, at my husband, at me again, then, with a half-smile, clarified, "Nonalcoholic?"

Blushing, I nodded. "Yes, please."

She nodded and, as she scribbled on her order pad, said, "Sometimes you can just tell."

Needless to say, we left a very generous tip for our very observant waitress.

Reading My X ray

CHRIS CROWE

I am a victim of advancing age. Not that long ago, I had extreme difficulty understanding why newspapers published obituaries. Now I read them looking for deceased who are younger than I am. Now I read, and am interested in, articles about the prostate, a dumb little organ I didn't even know existed two or three years ago. And I worry—about cholesterol, salt, and fat; about secondhand smoke and ultraviolet rays; about drunk drivers and gun-toting lunatics; about life insurance and mortgages; about the kids and college and missions and marriages. And, of course, I worry that I worry too much.

It's made me into something of a pessimist, though I hardly think of myself that way. But an experience this morning, another middle-aged indignity, made it pretty clear that when it comes to my health, I tend to see the glass as half-empty.

It was an IVP, an intravenous pyelograph examination, a surprisingly painless dye and X ray kind of thing. But it has an ominous purpose: identifying little nuggets of junk that might be clogging important organs or tracts, marking organs that are inflamed or flabby, diagnosing malignant things inside. When the test was nearly finished, I was told to use the rest room before the final series of X rays. On my way to the rest room, I passed through the X-ray reading room and saw my kidneys up on the light board. I immediately wished I hadn't. There, in the lower right-hand corner of each X ray, appeared a sinister dark spot.

My knees weakened and my hands turned cold.

When I climbed back up on the X-ray table, Liz, who, kind and supportive wife that she is, had stayed at my side through this most recent trial, asked me why I looked so pale.

"I saw my X rays," I said. "There's a dark spot on the bladder or kidney or something. It doesn't look good."

Her eyes widened and she bit her lip. We were both scared more than before, but she assured me it was probably nothing. I appreciated her optimism but was certain I'd just seen my tumor. My optimism hoped it would turn out to be benign.

When the exam was over, the technician came in and announced that no kidney stones had shown up, no abnormal organs were revealed, no blockages discovered. Everything looked clear and normal. It had merely been an infection.

Yeah, right. He's just letting my doctor tell me about the tumor. Professional courtesy.

After I had changed back into my clothes, I found Liz in the X-ray reading room looking at my X rays with the technician. He was pointing out this and that, where the dye had been and what it revealed.

Then she asked about the ominous dark spot.

"Oh, that?" he said, tapping my tumor with his index finger. "That's just gas."

Rescued

RICHARD PETERSON

While making my rounds as a traveling sales-
man one day, I had lunch at a McDonald's, then pulled
my car into a residential street near the restaurant to
take a short nap. I parked at the curb, laid my seat back,
and quickly dozed off.

I was enjoying a peaceful snooze when I was awakened by the loud sound of an engine idling nearby. I
opened my eyes to find a fire truck parked next to my
car. Standing on the other side of the street was a
woman holding her hand over her mouth and staring at
me with a worried expression on her face.

At that moment, an ambulance, with *four* paramedics
in the front seat, pulled around the corner and stopped
in front of the fire engine. As the paramedics were piling
out of the cab, a fireman wearing full fire-fighting regalia
jumped out of the truck and rapped on my driver's side
car window. When I rolled it down, he asked, "Are you
okay?"

Except for the embarrassment I was feeling at having
been mistaken for dead, I was perfectly fine.

When I responded to the fireman that I had just been taking a nap, he turned to the other would-be rescuers and called out loudly, "I saved him!" I took that as my signal to start my car and sheepishly drive away.

Luke Skywalker

KATHLEEN "CASEY" NULL

I was pushing Christopher on the swing as he proclaimed, "Higher! Higher!"

Then he said he wanted to go high enough "to see Luke Skywalker!"

I pushed him higher and soon he exclaimed, "I see him! I see Luke Skywalker!" I replied with my usual, "Uh-huh," assuming he was fantasizing about space flight and *Star Wars*. Then I found myself lost in thought about children's wonderful imaginations until he interrupted my reverie.

"Can you see Luke Skywalker, Mommy?"

"No, can you?"

"Yeah! He's right there on the roof. I threw him up there!"

Sure enough, there was a little plastic action figure on the roof.

Not a Stroke After All

DOUGLAS COLTON PERRY

*T*en years ago, Janice and I were in Cuzco, Peru, which is 12,000 feet above sea level. At 12,000 feet you get headaches and can't think straight—you do funny things. We were with our son (who had just completed his mission) in a hotel room with three single beds and lamp tables between. We said our prayers and tried hard to get to sleep. During the night I heard a terrible cry, "Honey, please come quick. I think I'm having a stroke." I sat bolt upright with a gallon of adrenaline tearing through my system. I ran down the hall to the bathroom, looked in—and laughed. There was my sweetheart having a stroke, and all I could do was laugh. That's awful. I said, "I'll be right back." I raced back into the room, grabbed what I needed, went back to the bathroom door, and said encouragingly, "Sweetheart, if you'll take *my* glasses off and put *your* glasses on, I think the stroke will go away."

Bogus Brigham

BRIGHAM YOUNG

I do not profess to be much of a joker, but I do think this to be one of the best jokes ever perpetrated. By the time we were at work in the Nauvoo Temple, officiating in the ordinances, the mob had learned that "Mormonism" was not dead, as they had supposed. We had completed the walls of the Temple, and the attic story from about halfway up of the first windows, in about fifteen months. It went up like magic, and we commenced officiating in the ordinances. Then the mob commenced to hunt for other victims; they had already killed the Prophets Joseph and Hyrum in Carthage jail, while under the pledge of the State for their safety, and now they wanted Brigham, the President of the Twelve Apostles, who were then acting as the Presidency of the Church.

I was in my room in the Temple; it was in the southeast corner of the upper story. I learned that a posse was lurking around the Temple, and that the United States Marshal was waiting for me to come down, whereupon I knelt down and asked my Father in heaven, in the name of Jesus, to guide and protect me that I might live to prove advantageous to the Saints. Just as I arose from my knees and sat down in my chair, there came a rap at my door. I said, "Come in," and Brother George D. Grant, who was then engaged driving my carriage and doing chores for me, entered the room.

Said he, "Brother Young, do you know that a posse and the United States Marshal are here?" I told him I had heard so. On entering the room Brother Grant left the door open. Nothing came into my mind what to do, until looking directly across the hall I saw Brother William Miller leaning against the wall.

As I stepped towards the door I beckoned to him; he came. Said I to him, "Brother William, the Marshal is here for me; will you go and do just as I tell you? If you will, I will serve them a trick." I knew that Brother Miller was an excellent man, perfectly reliable and capable of carrying out my project. Said I, "Here, take my cloak;" but it happened to be Brother Heber C. Kimball's; our cloaks were alike in color, fashion, and size. I threw it around his shoulders, and told him to wear my hat and accompany Brother George D. Grant. He did so. I said to Brother Grant, "George, you step into the carriage and look towards Brother Miller, and say to him, as though you were addressing me, 'Are you ready to ride?' You can do this, and they will suppose Brother Miller to be me, and proceed accordingly," which they did.

Just as Brother Miller was entering the carriage, the Marshal stepped up to him, and, placing his hand upon his shoulder, said, "You are my prisoner." Brother William entered the carriage and said to the Marshal,

"I am going to the Mansion House, won't you ride with me?" They both went to the Mansion House. There were my sons Joseph A., Brigham Jr., and Brother Heber C. Kimball's boys, and others who were looking on, and all seemed at once to understand and partake of the joke. They followed the carriage to the Mansion House and gathered around Brother Miller, with tears in their eyes, saying, "Father, or President Young, where are you going?" Brother Miller looked at them kindly, but made no reply; and the Marshal really thought he had got "Brother Brigham."

Lawyer Edmonds, who was then staying at the Mansion House, appreciating the joke, volunteered to Brother Miller to go to Carthage with him and see him safe through. When they arrived within two or three miles of Carthage, the Marshal with his posse stopped. They arose in their carriages, buggies, and wagons, and, like a tribe of Indians going into battle, or as if they were a pack of demons, yelling and shouting, they exclaimed, "We've got him! We've got him! We've got him!"

When they reached Carthage the Marshal took the supposed Brigham into an upper room of the hotel and placed a guard over him, at the same time telling those around that he had got him. Brother Miller remained in the room until they bid him come to supper. While there, parties came in, one after the other, and asked for Brigham. Brother Miller was pointed out to them. So it continued, until an apostate Mormon, by the name of Thatcher, who had lived in Nauvoo, came in, sat down and asked the landlord where Brigham Young was. The landlord, pointing across the table to Brother Miller, said, "That is Mr. Young." Thatcher replied, "Where? I can't see any one that looks like Brigham." The landlord told him it was that fat, fleshy man eating. "Oh, h___!" exclaimed Thatcher, "that's not Brigham; that is William Miller, one of my old neighbors."

Upon hearing this the landlord went and, tapping the Sheriff on the shoulder, took him a few steps to one side, and said, "You have made a mistake, that is not Brigham Young; it is William Miller, of Nauvoo." The Marshal, very much astonished, exclaimed, "Good heavens! and *he* passed for Brigham." He then took Brother Miller into a room, and, turning to him, said, "What in h___ is the reason you did not tell me your name?"

Brother Miller replied, "You have not asked me my name."

"Well," said the Sheriff, with another oath, "What is your name?"

"My name," he replied, "is William Miller."

Said the Marshal, "I thought your name was Brigham Young. Do you say this for a fact?"

"Certainly I do," said Brother Miller.

"Then," said the Marshal, "why did you not tell me this before?"

"I was under no obligations to tell you," replied Brother Miller, "as you did not ask me."

Then the Marshal, in a rage, walked out of the room, followed by Brother Miller, who walked off in company with Lawyer Edmonds, Sheriff Backenstos, and others, who took him across lots to a place of safety; and this is the real pith of the story of "Bogus" Brigham, as far as I can recollect.

Scout Camp Postcard from the Nudist Ranch

JEFF SHEETS

*M*y most memorable experience at Scout camp took place in the Uintah Mountains east of Salt Lake City. On the way to our camp we passed by the Beaver Creek Nudist Ranch and its extra-large-hand-waving-smiling-bear-mascot billboard as you pass it on the highway.

The instant we passed the sign, my Scoutmaster, ever the jokester, pulled his van off the road and stopped. The rest of the caravan of cars pulled over too. We huddled up, and within a few minutes all of us boys had taken off our shirts and shoes and socks, and had wrapped our towels around our shorts-covered waists. We all posed by the billboard and gave our best imitation of the big bear waving "Hi" to our families at home.

Photos were taken, and you can imagine my mother's surprise when she received the postcard of a group of 30 Scouts, clothed in nothing but towels and smiles, waving in front of the Beaver Creek Nudist Ranch, with the handwritten letter—"Having a GREAT time at camp! Love, your son!"

Hamster Day

TOM HEWITSON

$\mathcal{T}$he new millennium has brought with it a lot of new and exciting interests and hobbies for my two daughters. Natalie, age five, has become completely enamored with collecting the newly minted series of quarters, and quickly places each in her "fancy quarter book" whenever she gets a new one. Seven-year-old Alyssa has discovered a great love for animals and as our little nurturer, cares for a variety of neighborhood pets and critters. Each of the girls feeds off of the other's interests, and my wife and I support their interests wholeheartedly. We did, that is, until the day we now call "Hamster Day."

Hamster Day happened on a Saturday and began like most any other. The day's events included such chores as doing yard work and grocery shopping. We anticipated the evening, when we were planning to visit my parents, Grandpa and Grandma "BooWoo"—named appropriately by Alyssa after their dog. A couple of hours prior to our departure, Natalie commented that she had called Grandpa BooWoo and had been told that "he has a new hamster for me!"

Imagine our dismay. Dogs? Okay. Cats? Maybe. But hamsters? I was quickly taken back to my youth when I had had several not-so-pleasant experiences with hamsters. Apprehensively, we were soon on our way. All Natalie could talk about was her new hamster. I drove very slowly. Then the much anticipated moment came as we entered the driveway. Standing there to greet us were Mom and Dad—but no hamster. "Great," I thought, "probably in some little smelly box with a bunch of half-eaten lettuce and carrots." Mom took us into the house, where we enjoyed a fine visit—but still no hamster. Suddenly, the high-pitched voice of our youngest cut through the moment as she ran into the room yelling, "My new hamster! My new hamster!"

There in her little hand was a shiny new quarter from New Hampshire for her "fancy quarter book."

Using Your Noodle

ELAINE CANNON

My father was a great storyteller and always had a quick line to soften a tense situation. I well remember when my mother was first learning to drive. It was very exciting for all of us. One day Dad came home from work to learn that Mother had crunched a fender and curled the running board on the garage door as she'd tried to back out.

At the table he said: "Well, children, your mother's had herself a day. Tangling with a garage door can injure your pride. But that's nothing to what happened yesterday in traffic. She stalled the car and a policeman came over to scold her into moving along because she was hindering the flow of traffic.

"'I can't,' cried Mother. 'I don't remember what to do.' [Mother was never very calm under pressure.]

"'Well, use your noodle, lady! Use your noodle.'

"'Where is it? Where is it? I've tried every gadget I can find.'"

Oh, Sure, It's Funny Now . . .

Up in the Night

CHRIS SCHOEBINGER

*M*y aunt and uncle, who are just turning seventy, recently took a vacation cruise. It was very early one morning when my uncle got out of bed to use the bathroom. Sleepy, and in unfamiliar surroundings, he became disoriented. Instead of going through the bathroom door in his cabin, he went out the front door and into the main corridor. The door closed behind him, and he just kept walking. In a matter of seconds he realized where he was and what he was wearing—only his underwear! He quickly backed up but was unsure which cabin door was his. He couldn't remember his room number, and only half-dressed, he didn't dare knock on a stranger's door at 2:00 A.M.

He waited in the corridor for nearly an hour, half-hoping that someone would come along who could help, half-hoping no one would see him. Finally, he went down to the elevator and used the emergency phone inside. He told the person who answered, "I've locked myself out of my cabin, and I don't know which one is mine. By the way, I'm not dressed very modestly. Will you please send someone down right away?"

After what seemed a long time, someone came to help him, and my uncle was greatly relieved to get back in his room, though he could just imagine what the ship's attendant said when he got back to his station: "Have I got a story for you . . ."

My aunt slept through the whole thing.

Please, Pass the Salt

LORI BOYER

*F*or me, humor is the WD40™ in the grind of everyday life. Humor rescues me from friction in countless crucial ways. First, I find humor can diffuse the tension and douse the sparks in very volatile situations. My husband will always be grateful to a man who saved him with humor from a terribly embarrassing incident.

Richard had been invited to his high-school girlfriend's home for a formal, no-holds-barred, linen-and-fine-china Sunday dinner. For a teenage boy, girlfriends' fathers and fine china are unwelcome prospects. But he really liked this girl and recognized the significance of the invitation. He wanted to make a good impression, so he dressed up, sought a briefing from his mother on dinner etiquette, and arrived at his girlfriend's house reasonably well-prepared.

The whole family was there, a large family. He was the only guest. After the blessing on the food, the girl's father turned to my future husband and said, "Richard, please pass the salt and pepper."

Richard, praying that no one would notice his hand

213

was shaking, picked up the crystal salt and pepper shakers, reached out to hand them to the father, but instead dropped them into a goblet of ice water. To his horror, the goblet shattered, spilling water everywhere.

A long painful silence ensued during which Richard fervently wished to disappear. Then the father said amiably, "Richard, please pass the salt water."

The Third Loaf

DENNIS GAUNT

*W*hen I was fourteen, I found myself in a peculiar situation. Curiously, even though we were living in a large, thriving ward in the heart of the Church, I was the only young man in my age group. I *was* the teachers quorum.

Two things were impressed on me: first, with so many people in the ward, we would need plenty of bread and water for the sacrament each Sunday; second, since I was the teachers quorum, that duty would fall to me every week.

Our ward met at nine o'clock in the morning, and I soon learned that in order to have the sacrament prepared before everyone showed up for church, I would have to arrive at least an hour earlier. It was also customary for the ward that met first to bring enough bread for the other ward that met in our building.

And so it was that every week, I begrudgingly trudged out my door and down to the chapel with three loaves of bread in hand—two for us, and one for the other ward. Every week I prepared what seemed like bushels

215

of bread and gallons of water for our ward. Every week I left my third loaf under the sacrament table for the teachers in the other ward to use. And every week nobody from either ward ever said thank-you or acknowledged my efforts.

It really began to bother me. I thought: *Why should I bring this other loaf for them? Why can't they bring their own?* I made a decision. I was going to do something I had never done before. I was going to be rebellious. If the other ward wasn't going to thank me, then they could get their own bread!

The following Sunday, I made my usual preparations, but this time I brought only two loaves of bread. Our sacrament meeting came and went without a hitch. Later, as I was walking out of my teachers quorum meeting, I noticed a large crowd gathered in the foyer of the building. They were all peering into the chapel and listening intently. I walked over, peeked inside, and saw what everyone was looking at. A sister in that ward had written a biography about President Ezra Taft Benson, and he had decided to pay her sacrament meeting a surprise visit. There he stood at the pulpit, bearing his testimony. I was so excited at seeing the prophet that any thought of my earlier rebellion vanished from my memory. I listened, thrilled, and then ran home to tell my parents what I had just seen and heard.

My dad waited for me to finish, and then he turned to my mother and said, "Did you hear what else happened at that meeting? No sacrament bread. The bishop had to send his wife home for a loaf so they could give the sacrament to the prophet." He then turned to me. "You wouldn't happen to know anything about that, would you?"

I stood speechless, mouth agape, sputtering and stammering for something to say. If my eyes had gotten any wider, I would've been able to see the back of my head. My father let a small smile escape, knowing he wouldn't have to pursue the matter further, and then left the room.

I never failed in my duty again.

Slipping at the Temple

TONYA-RAE FACEMYER

$\mathcal{I}$was living and working in Provo when one of my younger brothers was at the Missionary Training Center, preparing for his mission. He had received permission to meet me at the Provo Temple so we could attend an endowment session together. We were going to catch the first session of the day, which meant getting to the temple around 6:00 A.M.

It had snowed heavily during the night and getting to the temple took longer than I had thought. When I arrived, the temple parking lot had not yet been plowed and was very slick. I parked my car and got out and immediately fell, hard. I quickly looked around to see if anyone had noticed my less-than-graceful fall and noticed another woman slip and fall.

I got myself up and took two steps and fell again. I tried to grab hold of the car as I went down but failed. A nice gentleman had noticed both my falls and the trouble the other woman was having and shouted to us to stay put. He helped her into the temple, then came and got me and escorted me in as well.

Inside the temple a sweet temple worker noticed that my knee was bleeding and offered to help clean and bandage the wound. After receiving the first aid, I knew I was running late and quickly changed clothes and proceeded to the chapel.

Because of the delays, I missed the first session, and my brother. Discouraged, I sat in the back of the chapel and cried. A few minutes later my brother walked in. He was running late because his companion had not been excited about getting up that early on his P-day and walking in the snow to the temple. It had taken him a while to find a missionary who wanted to come with him. I was glad he had persevered and that we were able to go through a session together.

After the temple session was finished and I had gone to work I began to ache all over. My arm hurt, my neck hurt, and my knee was killing me, so I decided to go to the hospital and get checked out. As it turned out the two falls in the parking lot of the temple had caused a bit of damage. I had broken my arm, jammed some muscles in my neck, and had to have ten stitches in my knee.

A few days later, when I met my brother at the airport to see him off to Montana, he was shocked! I was wearing a neck brace, a cast on my arm, and a large bandage covering the stitches on my knee, the aftereffects of our early morning temple excursion.

Spotlight on Talmadge

LINDA J. EYRE

*O*ur family was at the open-air, hillside theater at the Sundance Summer Theater, awaiting the start of *The Sound of Music*. Our seven-year-old son, Talmadge, needed to go to the bathroom. It was getting dark, and I sent him off into the woods to take care of the problem. What Talmadge didn't realize was that just as he "opened fire" in a grove of trees on the mountainside, the spotlight that had fallen on Maria singing "The hills are alive with the sound of music" also fell on him. He was totally oblivious; but the audience was in hysterics. We sure hoped he couldn't find us until after dark, as he made his way back through the tittering crowd.

Stuck at Mammoth Cave

EMILY BENNETT WATTS

$\mathscr{F}$or a few months while we were engaged, my future husband lived in Cedar City and I lived in Salt Lake City. One week my family traveled down to Cedar City to attend the Shakespeare Festival and also to give me a chance to see him. During this trip, he took us to Mammoth Cave, which isn't a cave like Timpanogos or Carlsbad Caverns with beautiful rock formations and tour guides. It might more aptly have been named "Mammoth Hole in the Ground." You climb down into the mouth of it on your own with flashlights. The tunnel, a little lava flow, gets progressively smaller and narrower until you come out of the cave at the other end. He thought it would be an adventure for us, so in we climbed: my parents, my brothers, my fiancé, and I.

Being somewhat cautious and not at all surefooted, I was the last one to get through the cave, and when I finally got to the climbing-out part, I got stuck. My husband-to-be stood outside Mammoth Cave and laughed and laughed and laughed. That sounds unchivalrous, maybe even mean, but it would have been meaner for him to come over and say, "Oh, my goodness, oh, my gosh, what are we going to do?" I was having visions of Winnie the Pooh, being stuck there until I thinned out enough that they could pop me out. Because he was laughing, the pressure was off, and I felt confident that there must be a solution. Sure enough, my kind younger brother assessed the situation and instructed me how to untangle my feet and my legs so that I could wriggle out of Mammoth Cave and carry on with my life.

The Singing Toilet

LINDA J. EYRE

$\mathcal{O}$ne summer we had an opportunity to take our children to Japan. It was an amazing experience! John and Susan, the wonderful couple who invited us to stay with them for a whole month, had not had a family of their own and wanted to learn what it would be like to have one. I think they got more of an experience than they bargained for. Even though everything else in Japan seemed tiny, their house was enormous by Japanese standards. We had one tatami room (an empty room with straw mats for sleeping) for the girls and one for the boys. Richard and I slept on a thicker mat in an 8- by 10-foot room.

Things were outrageously expensive in Japan. The rent on their house was $12,000 per month. Luckily, John and Susan only had to pay the first $1,000, and his company covered the rest. Carrots, apples, and oranges were at least $1.00 each. Watermelons were about $50. We once saw a 14-inch square box of beautiful cherries, lined up to perfection, that sold for $125.

One of the funny things for an American in Japan is

the strange translation of Japanese words into English. They called McDonald's MacDonal'dos. The marketplace was full of T-shirts on which were printed unintelligible clumps of unrelated English words.

One day our wonderful hostess asked if I would like to go with her on her weekly trip to the chiropractor. My back was aching, and she wanted him to have a look at it. I had never been to a chiropractor, but thought it would be an adventure. We took a train and a bus and walked up a long hill to a large house that was the chiropractor's office. The waiting room was a fairly large living room, and the bedrooms off of the main room were the examining rooms. As we arrived I realized that I had drunk a lot of water and was in desperate need of a rest room. While Susan waited I was directed to a tiny room in the corner of the big waiting room, obviously added for patrons after the house was bought for doctoring purposes. It was just big enough for me to fit in. In fact, I had to lean over the toilet to shut the door. There was a control panel, filled with lights and buttons, in the tiny room. Below one button was some Japanese and underneath that what appeared to be an English translation that said, "Singing Toilet." I was dying to know what would happen if I pushed that button, but I calculated that it would be pretty embarrassing if I pushed it and it started wailing out some wild Japanese music through the paper-thin walls, so I stifled the urge.

As I faced the toilet to flush it, I leaned over to look at the "singing toilet" button one more time. I just couldn't resist the urge to know what the toilet would "sing."

When I pushed the button, a stream of water shot out at me with the same pressure as a fire hose and hit me directly in the crotch. I was so startled that it took me a few seconds to register what had even happened. I frantically tried to push other buttons to make it stop; but the steady stream was relentless. I couldn't move to the right or the left to get out of its path, and I knew that if I opened the door, not only would I get the back of my pants drenched as well, but the water would shoot out into the waiting room. I was trying not to scream, as the waiting room was full of demure Japanese folks who were already "bent out of shape." All I could do was wait for the stream (obviously intended to be some sort of fancy bidet) to stop. When it finally petered out, I looked down at myself and saw an enormous amount of water on the front of my pants that could only mean one thing to the people in the waiting room. I couldn't wait. I sat on the toilet and laughed until I cried. I cried and cried. (In fact, every time I tell this story I cry.)

How could I be that stupid? I thought. *Could the translator have meant "squirting" instead of "singing?"* (They both start with S.) *How am I going to go out into that waiting room looking like this?* I was shaking with laughter through my tears. After about five minutes, I got hold of myself, dried my eyes, and decided to take off my sweatshirt and tie it around my waist with the big part in front. It came almost down to my knees. It looked sort of strange, but not nearly as strange as the water stain looked on my khaki pants. I couldn't explain my dilemma to the doctor because he didn't speak much English, and he must have thought my outfit very odd as he checked out my back. I hoped he just chalked it up to weird American fashions. That's a day I'll never forget!

Duet in Texas

RANDAL WRIGHT

I was sitting on the stand next to the stake president during a session of youth conference in Texas. At one point in the program a youth choir gathered on the stand to sing. The group stood directly in front of us and began a hymn. It was supposed to be a mixed chorus, but there were only three young men among a large group of young women in the choir. The stake president, who loved to sing, was obviously concerned that the young men were outnumbered, and to give them some additional volume, he quickly opened his hymn book and began singing along. He soon motioned to me to join in singing with him.

We remained seated and sang quite softly at first. But it was obvious that the girls were drowning out the young men, so we increased our volume, trying our best to help out. By the time we came to the third verse, the president and I were really into our new roles, and we started out strongly.

Imagine our chagrin when we discovered that the choir had quit singing while the pianist was playing an interlude between the second and third verses. The unannounced duet coming from behind the choir caused quite a stir.

Sources and Permissions

A Time to Laugh

"When Zucchini Happens . . ." by Joseph Walker, from *How Can You Mend a Broken Spleen?* (Salt Lake City: Shadow Mountain, 1998), 13–15.

"When Several Days Attack You at Once" by Janene Baadsgaard, from *Families Who Laugh . . . Last* (Salt Lake City: Deseret Book, 1992), 22–24.

"OD'd on Shrimp" by Tom Plummer, from *Eating Chocolates and Dancing in the Kitchen* (Salt Lake City: Shadow Mountain, 1998), 127–30.

"Self-esteem" by Marilynne Linford, from *A Woman Fulfilled* (Salt Lake City: Bookcraft, 1992), 57–58.

"The Geezer in the Glass" by Joseph Walker, from *How Can You Mend a Broken Spleen?* (Salt Lake City: Shadow Mountain, 1998), 102–4.

"Meeting Miss America" by JoAnn Peterson, previously unpublished.

"Who's Next?" by Shauna Gibby, previously unpublished.

"The Optimist," author unknown, in *Best-Loved Poems of the American People* (New York: Doubleday, 1936), 486.

229

"Home Improvement" by Tom Plummer, from *Eating Chocolates and Dancing in the Kitchen* (Salt Lake City: Shadow Mountain, 1998), 29–35.

"God Save the King!" by Mary Ellen Edmunds, from *Happiness: Finders, Keepers* (Salt Lake City: Deseret Book, 1999), 145–46.

"A Moment of Fame" by Robert Farrell Smith, previously unpublished.

"Driving from a Wheelchair" by Art E. Berg, from *Finding Peace in Troubled Waters* (Salt Lake City: Deseret Book, 1995), 100.

"'Welcome Back, Stupid!'" by Mary Ellen Edmunds, from *Happiness: Finders, Keepers* (Salt Lake City: Deseret Book, 1999), 41–42.

"Elevator Icebreaker" by Mary Ellen Edmunds, from *Happiness: Finders, Keepers* (Salt Lake City: Deseret Book, 1999), 38–39.

"Tent Failure" by Randal Wright, previously unpublished.

"Alzheimer's Pop Quiz" by Tom Plummer, *Eating Chocolates and Dancing in the Kitchen* (Salt Lake City: Shadow Mountain, 1998), 152–53.

"In Good Company!" by Mike Giesbrecht, previously unpublished.

"Lost Election" by Edgar A. Guest, from the *American Magazine*, in "Mutual Messages," *Improvement Era*, vol. 39, No. 2, February 1936.

"Jailhouse Prayer" by Jack R. Christianson, *Be Strong and of Good Courage* (Salt Lake City: Bookcraft, 1994), 76–77.

"Brother Perfect" by Pat Fairbanks, previously unpublished

"To Sing or Not to Sing!" by Robert Bean, previously unpublished.

Love and Laughter

"The Case for the Tried and True" by Joseph Walker, *How Can You Mend a Broken Spleen?* (Salt Lake City: Shadow Mountain, 1998), 233–36.

"Love and Basketball" by Douglas Colton Perry, in *May Christ Lift Thee Up* (Salt Lake City: Deseret Book, 1999), 248.

"My First Kiss" by Lisa Mangum, previously unpublished.

"Making the 'D'wight' Choice" by Dwight Durrant, in *Forward with Faith* (Salt Lake City: Deseret Book, 2000), 40–41.

"A Wish," in *Improvement Era*, vol. 2, No. 2, December 1898.

"Baking Bread" by Douglas Colton Perry, in *May Christ Lift Thee Up* (Salt Lake City: Deseret Book, 1999), 249–50.

We're All in This Together

"Quieting the Chaos" by Scott Hixson, previously unpublished.

"Don't Nuke Those Squirrels!" by Joseph Walker, *How Can You Mend a Broken Spleen?* (Salt Lake City: Shadow Mountain, 1998), 137–39.

"Unconventional Dinner" by Lori Boyer, in *Clothed with Charity,* eds. Dawn Hall Anderson, Susette Fletcher

231

Green, and Dlora Hall Dalton (Salt Lake City: Deseret Book, 1997), 87.

"Do You Remember When?" by Joseph Walker, *How Can You Mend a Broken Spleen?* (Salt Lake City: Shadow Mountain, 1998), 6–9.

"The Little Plumbers" by Chris Crowe, *Fatherhood, Football, and Turning Forty* (Salt Lake City: Bookcraft, 1995), 40–42.

"Mystery of the Missing Coat" by Emily Bennett Watts, in *Arise and Shine Forth* (Salt Lake City: Deseret Book, 2000), 192–93.

"Practicing for Christmas" by Richard Moore, previously unpublished.

"Peace on Earth" by Scott Hixson, previously unpublished.

"Santa Claus Calling" by Richard Moore, previously unpublished.

"Grandpa's Greatest Shot" by Lisa Mangum, previously unpublished.

"$90 Apricots" by Heather Pack, previously unpublished.

"Missing Death Date" by Mary Ellen Edmunds, from *Happiness: Finders, Keepers* (Salt Lake City: Deseret Book, 1999), 57.

Families Are Forever . . . Is That Some Kind of Threat?

"Lecture #3" by Lori Boyer, in *Clothed with Charity,* eds. Dawn Hall Anderson, Susette Fletcher Green, and Dlora Hall Dalton (Salt Lake City: Deseret Book, 1997), 88.

"Too Many Kids—Not Enough Drugs" by Brad Wilcox, in *Joy in the Journey* (Salt Lake City: Deseret Book, 1998), 81–82.

"I Love My Dad" by Randal Wright, previously unpublished.

"IRS-2K Form, No Kidding" by Terri Winder, previously unpublished.

"You Tell Me" by Eileen R. Yeager, previously unpublished.

"Bath Time for Bozos" by Janene Baadsgaard, from *Families Who Laugh . . . Last* (Salt Lake City: Deseret Book, 1992), 74–75.

"Joseph Fielding Receives a Whipping" by Joseph Fielding Smith, from Joseph F. McConkie, *True and Faithful: The Life Story of Joseph Fielding Smith* (Salt Lake City: Bookcraft, 1971), 19–20.

"Excuses, Excuses" by Lynn C. Jaynes, previously unpublished.

"Overflowing Bathtub" by Linda J. Eyre, from *Joyful Mother of Children* (Salt Lake City: Shadow Mountain, 2000), 139–42.

"Locked in the Bathroom" by Chris Crowe, from *Fatherhood, Football, and Turning Forty* (Salt Lake City: Bookcraft, 1995), 20–23.

Out of the Mouths of Babes

"101 to 97" by Randal Wright, previously unpublished.

"'Good Job, Dad!'" by Virginia U. Jensen, in *The Arms of His Love* (Salt Lake City: Deseret Book, 2000), 319.

"Super Bowl Winners?" by Melody Malone, previously unpublished.

"Tone of Voice" by Randal Wright, previously unpublished.

"Yea! He's Dead!" by Marni Hall, previously unpublished.

"Free Agency?" by Kerry Griffin Smith, previously unpublished.

"Joseph Smith Was Where!" by Claris Butler, previously unpublished.

"Earplugs" by Charri Jensen, previously unpublished.

"Still Counting . . . " by Sharon Sawyer, previously unpublished

"Baptized by the Dead" by DeLayna Barr, previously unpublished.

"The Voice of the Holy Ghost" by Tina Guay, previously unpublished.

Leaders and Laughter

"'Don't You Squeeze Me!'" by Edward L. Kimball and Andrew E. Kimball Jr., *Spencer W. Kimball* (Salt Lake City: Bookcraft, 1977), 333.

"Ida's Hearing" by F. Burton Howard, adapted from *Marion G. Romney: His Life and Faith* (Salt Lake City: Bookcraft, 1988), 144–45.

"'I Was in Hopes You Wouldn't Recognize Me'" by Francis M. Gibbons, *Spencer W. Kimball: Resolute Disciple, Prophet of God* (Salt Lake City: Deseret Book, 1995), 290–91.

"Japanese Courtesy" by David O. McKay, from *Home Memories of President David O. McKay,* comp., Llewelyn R. McKay (Salt Lake City: Deseret Book, 1956), 45–46.

"Brigham Young's Spelling" by James B. Allen, Ronald K. Esplin, and David J. Whittaker, *Men with a Mission, 1837–1841: The Quorum of the Twelve Apostles in the British Isles* (Salt Lake City: Deseret Book, 1992), 157–58.

"'Where's the Siren?'" by Lucile C. Tate, *Boyd K. Packer: A Watchman on the Tower* (Salt Lake City: Bookcraft, 1995), 42.

"A Get-Well Wish" by Carlos E. Asay, *Family Pecan Trees* (Salt Lake City: Deseret Book, 1992), 100.

"Property Poem" by Joseph Fielding Smith, *Life of Joseph F. Smith* (Salt Lake City: Deseret Book, 1938), 21.

"Singing vs. Snoring" by Elaine Cannon, *Bedtime Stories for Grownups* (Salt Lake City: Bookcraft, 1988), 148–49.

"Brigham's Interpretation" by Daniel Harrington, *Improvement Era*, vol. 31, No. 2, February 1938.

Missionaries and Mirth

"Letter from West Africa" by Mary Ellen Edmunds, in *Women Steadfast in Christ*, eds. Dawn Hall Anderson and Marie Cornwall (Salt Lake City: Deseret Book, 1992), 149–50.

"Tracting Woes" by Dennis Gaunt, previously unpublished.

"A Matter of Evidence" from "Wit and Humor in the Mission Field," in *Improvement Era*, vol. 8, No. 1, November 1904.

"A Sign-seeker Satisfied" from "Wit and Humor in the Mission Field," in *Improvement Era*, vol. 8, No. 1, November 1904.

"Parley Outruns the Dog" by Dean Hughes and Tom

Hughes, from *Great Stories from Mormon History* (Salt Lake City: Deseret Book, 1994), 23–27.

"They Understood Anyway" from "Wit and Humor in the Mission Field," in *Improvement Era,* vol. 8, No. 1, November 1904.

"A Matter of Perspective" by Shauna Gibby, previously unpublished.

"You Want *What* with Your Big Mac?" by Steve Gilchrist, previously unpublished.

"Pray with One Eye Open" by J. Golden Kimball, in Claude Richards, *J. Golden Kimball: The Story of a Unique Personality* (Salt Lake City: Deseret News Press, 1934), 48–49.

"A Holy Kiss" by James B. Allen, Ronald K. Esplin, and David J. Whittaker, from *Men with a Mission, 1837–1841: The Quorum of the Twelve Apostles in the British Isles* (Salt Lake City: Deseret Book Co., 1992), 159.

"When in Doubt, Don't Touch the Cat!" by Abbey Arndt, previously unpublished.

"Shotgun and Banana" by Jeff Johns, previously unpublished.

Misunderstandings, Mistakes, and Merriment

"Aunt Florence" by Mary Ellen Edmunds, in *Women Steadfast in Christ,* eds. Dawn Hall Anderson and Marie Cornwall (Salt Lake City: Deseret Book, 1992), 151–52.

"Golf High Jinks" by Richard Peterson, previously unpublished.

"'You Can Just Tell'" by Lisa Mangum, previously unpublished.

"Reading My X ray" by Chris Crowe, from *Fatherhood, Football, and Turning Forty* (Salt Lake City: Bookcraft, 1995), 10–11.

"Rescued" by Richard Peterson, previously unpublished.

"Luke Skywalker" by Kathleen "Casey" Null, from *Where Are We Going Besides Crazy?* (Salt Lake City: Bookcraft, 1989), 44–45.

"Not a Stroke After All" by Douglas Colton Perry, in *May Christ Lift Thee Up* (Salt Lake City: Deseret Book, 1999), 250.

"Bogus Brigham" by Brigham Young, from *Journal of Discourses*, 26 vols. (London: Latter-day Saints' Book Depot, 1854–86), 14:218–19.

"Scout Camp Postcard from the Nudist Ranch" by Jeff Sheets, previously unpublished.

"Hamster Day" by Tom Hewitson, previously unpublished.

"Using Your Noodle" by Elaine Cannon, from *Bedtime Stories for Grownups* (Salt Lake City: Bookcraft, 1988), 59–60.

Oh, Sure, It's Funny Now . . .

"Up in the Night" by Chris Schoebinger, previously unpublished.

"Please, Pass the Salt" by Lori Boyer, in *Clothed with Charity,* eds. Dawn Hall Anderson, Susette Fletcher Green, and Dlora Hall Dalton (Salt Lake City: Deseret Book, 1997), 86.

"The Third Loaf" by Dennis Gaunt, previously unpublished.

"Slipping at the Temple" by Tonya-Rae Facemyer, previously unpublished.

"Spotlight on Talmadge" by Linda J. Eyre, from *Joyful Mother of Children* (Salt Lake City: Shadow Mountain, 2000), 139–42.

"Stuck at Mammoth Cave" by Emily Bennett Watts, in *Arise and Shine Forth* (Salt Lake City: Deseret Book, 2000), 192–93.

"The Singing Toilet" by Linda J. Eyre, from *Joyful Mother of Children* (Salt Lake City: Shadow Mountain, 2000), 139–42.

"Duet in Texas" by Randal Wright, previously unpublished.